SUCCESSFUL SINGLE PARENTING

How To Books

FAMILY REFERENCE

SUCCESSFUL SINGLE PARENTING

How to combine bringing up children
with your other life goals

Mike Lilley

IT'S DIFFICULT BEING
BOTH MOTHER AND FATHER TO
THEM!

How To Books

Cartoons by Mike Flanagan.

British Library Cataloguing-in-Publication data
A catalogue record for this book is available from the British Library.

© Copyright 1996 by Michael Lilley.

First published in 1996 by How To Books Ltd, Plymbridge House, Estover Road, Plymouth PL6 7PZ, United Kingdom.
Tel: (01752) 202301. Fax: (01752) 202331.

Note: The material contained in this book is set out in good faith for general guidance and no liability can be accepted for loss or expense incurred as a result of relying in particular circumstances on statements made in the book. The laws and regulations are complex and liable to change, and readers should check the current position with the relevant authorities before making personal arrangements.

Produced for How To Books by Deer Park Productions.
Typeset by Kestrel Data, Exeter.
Printed and bound by Cromwell Press,
Broughton Gifford, Melksham, Wiltshire.

Contents

List of Illustrations

Lone parents become:	Lone parenting involves:
• able to manage change	• having a sense of humour
• good at managing money	• sharing
• independent	• having fun
• responsible	• working hard
• well organised	• fighting for what you believe in
• able to cope	• caring
• close to their children	• gaining control over your life
• good at making decisions	• seeing things through to the end

Foreword

The fear of the breakdown of traditional family values and the moral panic surrounding it have led to lone parents being blamed for all of society's ills. The media outrage has stereotyped lone parents as welfare scroungers who have babies solely to jump the housing queue. This hysteria is far from the real situation. Most lone parents do not become so by choice. According to many surveys including the government's own, 90 per cent of lone parents want to work and are unable to do so because they are caught in the benefit/poverty trap.

This situation was not that different in 1970 when Tessa Fothergill, the founder of Gingerbread, found herself alone with two small sons and nowhere to live. Her problems were compounded by the fact that if she didn't find suitable accommodation the Social Services Department were threatening to take her children into care. The shame of this situation was that it wasn't uncommon. Social Services at that time appeared to prefer to take the children into care, rather than help a lone parent find a roof over her head. Feeling isolated and angry over the situation she found herself in, Tessa wrote to a Sunday newspaper, telling her story and asking if there was anyone in the same situation who would like to get together to organise a better deal for lone parent families. Three hundred letters came in from all over the country and from this Gingerbread was formed to 'ginger' up the government for more 'bread' for lone parent families.

There are now 300 groups in England and Wales alone, with separate organisations in Scotland, Northern Ireland and Eire. Gingerbread's motto 'helping you, helps me' is still as relevant today, as Gingerbread is based on a self-help ethos. We recognise that there are limits to self-help, as the members involved have other aspects to their lives, such as children, education and employment, but we have found that members who received help when they needed it are so committed to being there to help those that follow, as a way of thanks, that they successfully manage to juggle all of these things.

The problems faced by lone parents today are very similar to those of the 1970s, that is, poverty, housing, employment, childcare and social exclusion. Many of the members of Gingerbread refer to it as their extended family, perhaps because of demographic trends which have resulted in the demise of the traditional extended family. Such demographic and social changes have led to the need for guides like Michael Lilley's on *Successful Single Parenting*. Michael's book is written with the understanding of someone who's been there himself, as Mike is a lone parent.

I would like to see a world where such guides were not necessary and where there was no need for an organisation like Gingerbread. In my Utopia, lone parents would be socially integrated into society and would be given the same opportunities and an equal standard of living. There are an awful lot of lone parents out there whose talents are being wasted, who could make a real contribution to society if they were given the chance. Guides and organisations such as Gingerbread are still needed as starting points and it is still a case of 'helping you, helps me'.

Carol Revell
Chairperson of Gingerbread
(*The national support organisation for lone parents in the UK*)

Preface

I became a single parent suddenly after my wife left during a family holiday in Majorca. One day I was the father in a mother/father team with three children, the next day I was classed as a single parent. The parent that had to take full responsibility. I was traumatised. Like many single parents, I never envisaged myself falling into this category. It was a whole new world, and an experience that I value but would have preferred to avoid. I had to make the best of it and that meant showing great resourcefulness.

I coped very badly in the first stages, whilst caring for three children under 6 and holding down a job. I fell into a second relationship through severe loneliness. Sadly it was a question of jumping from the frying pan into the fire. I had to dig myself out of a larger hole when this relationship failed, and I subsequently lost my job.

The day my ex-wife left I was like a pilot of a plane that was heading for a crash after losing the co-pilot. I used all my gut determination to keep the plane in the air, but failed to realise the fuel had run out. It was when I hit rock bottom that I realised that the most important people involved were the passengers, who were our children.

I had to rebuild our lives and it was at this time I started to observe the regular media and political criticisms of single parents. I felt deeply hurt and angry. The majority of single parents are women and as a male single parent I have learnt first hand how difficult it is raising children on your own, and I have a great respect for women who against the odds bring up their children. It is a very tiring, lonely and unrecognised job. Single parents deserve a deep respect.

My book is a guide to the ways and ideas that hopefully will enable other single parents to feel confident in themselves and realise that they are not alone. People who deride lone parents have never been through the experience, and if they had they would be more respectful.

The title *Successful Single Parenting* was chosen to emphasise the fact that what you are doing is already a success, and with belief in yourself you can fulfil your potential and dreams, however far away they may seem.

I hope that others who are not honoured with the title of single parent will get a better understanding of our issues and hopefully give the respect we deserve.

The book has been written from the real life experiences of many single parents and I wish to thank them all as there are too many to name.

The case studies used to illustrate the text are based on entirely fictional characters and situations, and any resemblance to living persons would be entirely coincidental.

Michael Lilley

1
Becoming a Single Parent

'I didn't want to be a single parent. I didn't want the stigma—seems odd now! Although I knew lots of single parents. I never thought I would end up in that position. Now, I'm proud to be a successful parent bringing up my children alone.'

The routes to single parenthood are wide and varied. In Britain today, single parents make up one in five families.

The one parent family is not a new phenomenon as lone parents have been here for a long time and will continue to be part of society, represented in all ethnic and age groups, classes and lifestyles.

Lone parents do face problems, mainly because our society is built around the idea that it is normal for two people to share in bringing up their children, and for one of the parents to look after them while the other goes out to earn the money. Lone parents have to do both these jobs. The viewpoint of this book is that a one parent family is a normal family unit, and trends indicate that this will become a predominant lifestyle for many of us.

Good parenting is to do with self-esteem, being well supported, having a good and happy environment. This is true of everyone, not just single parents. The more confidence you have in your parenting the more likely you are to cope with the ups and downs. It could be said that single parents are actually pioneering a new approach to parenting.

Whatever the route to lone parenthood, the issues that confront lone parents are the same:

● getting your benefits and tax sorted out

● seeking payment of child maintenance

● getting a secure place to live

- sorting out the separation or divorce

- planning to go back to work

- getting childcare arrangements sorted out

- planning some leisure time and holidays.

This book tackles all these issues.

WHAT MAKES A SINGLE PARENT A GOOD PARENT?

You will have your own definition of a good parent, but the key issue is that being a single parent does not mean that you are any worse or any better than a two parent family. Remember that:

- It is not quantity but quality of parenting that is important to a child.

- Parents in difficult circumstances need support, not hostility.

- Parenting success depends on support networks and financial security.

- A parent's emotional well-being affects the child's emotional well-being—your needs are linked, not separate.

HOW DO YOU FEEL AS A SINGLE PARENT?

It is not easy being a single parent and you will go through long periods of despair. Look at the box opposite and see how many of these feelings you have now or have had in the past.

LOOKING AT THE STATISTICS

A hard look at the facts of any situation is a good way to dispel any myths. Lone parents are portrayed by the press and some politicians as reckless teenage mums having numerous difficult children. The reality is that the huge increase in single parent families is linked to changes in our society, women's growing economic independence, attitudes towards relationships, and modern pressures of life.

Hurt   Disillusioned   Lonely   Strong   Out of love

Rejected   Nervous   Isolated   Free

Trapped   Angry   Displaced   In control   In debt

Withdrawn   Happy   Disenchanted   Stressed

Positive   Frightened   Outcast   Special

Tired   Forward looking   Hopeful   Depressed

No feelings   Numb   Joyful   Refreshed

Are the majority of single parents in the UK amongst the ethnic minorities?
No, 92 per cent of all lone parents are white. Just over 1 in 10 ethnic Asian families are headed by a lone mother. Over half the mothers in the Afro-Caribbean ethnic group were lone mothers in 1989–91.

Do unmarried single mothers have large families by numerous fathers?
No, while nearly 20 per cent of the lone mothers who had been married had three or more children, only 7 per cent of single lone unmarried mothers had three or more children.

Are there lots of teenage mums?
No, the average age at which women have their first baby is now 28 and it is increasingly likely that women will have their first baby in their thirties. The majority of lone mothers, over 60 per cent, are married women who are separated, divorced or widowed.

Single parent facts
- In 1992, there were 1.4 million one parent families in Great Britain with 2.2 million children.

- 21 per cent of all families with dependent children are now headed by a lone parent. The present growth is nearly 100,000 new single parent families per year.

- There will be over 2 million single parent families by the year 2000: 1 in 3 families.

- Lone fathers account for 10 per cent of the total and are a fast rising group as attitudes are changing, with courts giving more consideration to who is the best parent to care for the children and not automatically awarding custody to the mother.

- In 1992, families headed by a lone parent had on average 1.7 children, while married couples had on average 1.9 children.

- 1 out of 3 live births in the UK is outside marriage.

Is the single parent family becoming commonplace?
Like it or not, the traditional view of 'one mum, one dad, plus 2.6 children' is rapidly disappearing. It is now quite common for children to be brought up by single parents or to have one or more sets of step-parents.

Do people plan to be a single parent?
Sometimes, but it is important to note that even though Great Britain has the second highest rate of extramarital births in the European Union after Denmark, there is strong evidence that many of these births occur within stable relationships. Three-quarters of births outside marriage in 1992 were registered by both parents compared with only 45 per cent in 1971.

This shows that people do not start out with the intention of becoming a single parent, that the majority of children are born with the full knowledge and excitement of two parents, and that a variety of factors cause the break-ups in relationships resulting in one parent family situations. The increase of single parents throughout Europe is part of the huge change in attitudes towards relationships with more and more people rejecting the convention of marriage for life.

LEFT HOLDING THE BABY

'I thought having a baby would bring us closer together, but my fiancé decided he needed time to think about things and went to stay with his family. That was basically the last I saw of him.'

Historically, lone parents who have children outside marriage have had the hardest time. This group has so many different kinds of people in it. Most are women but some lone fathers now end up holding the baby.

This group represents lone parents who have had relationships that have broken up once pregnant, or just after the baby has been born.

Many feel that the arrival of the baby will ensure that the boyfriend will stay and a happy family life will result. All too often the man cannot cope and disappears with the full weight of parenthood falling upon the woman.

FACING SEPARATION AND DIVORCE

'I thought I was in a happy marriage when I accidentally discovered my wife was having an affair with my best friend. My life was shattered. We divorced two years later.'

The majority of one parent families are created as a result of separation and divorce. This route into lone parenthood can be very fraught. Parent and child alike may have experienced a good deal of pain in a separation and the parent may be trying to overcome bitterness in order to set up a positive relationship for the sake of the children. This can be very difficult.

Relationships break up for many reasons. The frequently used phrase 'unreasonable behaviour' covers many things from just growing apart to violence and/or infidelity.

EXPERIENCING BEREAVEMENT

'There was absolutely no advanced warning and when he died, it felt as if half of me had died with him, while the other half had to tell the children.'

In 1992, 6.35 per cent of lone parents in the UK were widows or widowers. There were 30,000 widowed lone fathers and 60,000 widowed lone mothers. They have to face the problems of single parenthood, while at the same time grieving for the death of their partner. Sometimes the death has happened suddenly and there is no time to prepare for single parenthood. It is just thrown at you. Other times, death has occurred after a traumatic long illness.

ESCAPING VIOLENCE AND ABUSE

'Basically as the violence grew worse I gave him an ultimatum that he had to change for the sake of the children. He didn't and I had to eventually escape the house when he was asleep.'

There are no national surveys of the extent of domestic violence, but the research that does exist shows that it is extensive although under-reported to the police. Some studies suggest that as many as 30 per cent of women have experienced violence from their partner. Some women stay with a violent partner for a prolonged period of time hoping that he will change. They may hate the violence but want the other things they think the relationship has to offer. They often finally flee with their children or have to get a court injunction to oust their estranged partner from the home.

CHOOSING TO HAVE A CHILD ON YOUR OWN

'It was a bit frightening but I suppose when you've got a baby all the time you've got to be the protective one. Sometimes, when he's in bed and I'm on my own I get a bit scared, but most of the time I'm fine.'

An increasing number of women in Britain are choosing to bring up their children on their own either because they have become pregnant by choice and decide to keep their babies and raise them without the involvement of the father, or because they have made a conscious decision to get pregnant and have a child. Although it is difficult to get a clear idea of exactly how many women are single mothers by choice, estimates are that they make up 10 per cent of the total of lone parents.

Some career women, fearful of the ticking of the biological time clock, decide to go ahead and have a child. Women in this position are still a very small percentage of the total and are often established in a well-paid job, can afford the costs of childcare, and have thought long and hard about what they are taking on and the change it will make to their lives.

The majority are women who have found themselves pregnant and decide to keep the baby and separate this issue from the relationship that created it. The days of having to marry the father have long gone.

CASE STUDIES—INTRODUCTION

Let us now introduce four single parents whose experiences we will be following in the succeeding chapters. Each has become a single parent through one of the outlined routes and they have tackled their life questions and problems in a variety of ways. All have experienced the issues covered in the following chapters and we will be able to observe how they and their children have established positive and fulfilling lives.

Sally Hunt brings up her son on her own

Sally is a 28-year-old single mum of Adam, aged 4. Sally lived with Brian, Adam's dad, for four years and they jointly bought a house. Sally worked as a clerk in an engineering company. When she became pregnant, Brian became distant and their relationship started to disintegrate. Just after the birth of Adam, Brian decided to leave. Sally had maternity leave from her job, but soon found it impossible to return, and decided to look after Adam full time and rely on state benefits. Sally now lives in local authority housing after her house was repossessed. Adam has no contact with his father. She attends college part time. 'As an unmarried parent I initially experienced some discrimination but having lived through the past four years, I am a much stronger person now and I can handle the ignorance. A lot of us are making the best of a situation we found ourselves in. We have taken on sole responsibility for our children, and often work harder to give them a decent, loving, normal home life.'

Martin Lewis is a single parent dad

Martin is a 40-year-old lone father of three children, Jane (15), Steven (11) and Mark (10). He has been on his own for eight years. Martin was married to Amanda for eight years, when suddenly she left through severe post-natal depression. She could not cope with looking after three small children and decided to go and live with her parents, initially to rest. She never returned and eventually they divorced. Martin worked full time as a manager of a security company, but because of the unsocial hours, had to give it up and rely on state benefit. He works part time in a youth club and is training to become a full time youth leader. Amanda visits the children regularly. Martin and Amanda have a strong friendship but have no intention of coming together again. 'It doesn't matter whether you are a man or a woman, you still face the same emotional problems and the loneliness. Whoever you are, the pleasure of being there for your kids is simply that of watching them grow up and seeing how they relate to you.'

Pamela Davis is a widow with two sons

Pamela is 35 and has two sons, Jason (12) and Wayne (7). Pam became a widow when her husband, David, died suddenly of a heart attack at the age of 30. Pam worked full time as a probation officer and has continued her job. She owns her own home. She had a boyfriend who moved in for a short time, but the relationship failed. She is seeing someone else now. 'Will we have to give up football mummy? How do you possibly answer a question like that from a little lad whose father has just died. That was what my son, Wayne, asked. People either sink or swim. No, I said, we won't be giving up football.'

Sue Chan has experienced divorce twice

Sue is 41 and has three children, Lucy (18), Elizabeth (6) and Michael (5). She has been married twice. Her first marriage ended in divorce after many years of violence. She met her second husband, Michael, through a single parent club. Their relationship lasted three years. Sue works part time as a school dinner nanny. Lucy has recently had a baby and lives with her mum. 'I hope my life is not finished. I see every morning as a beginning, the big element in life is fate. I've reached out to life as opposed to making life work for me. You get unhappy and frustrated if you have expectations and wants.'

DISCUSSION POINTS

1. How many single parents, other than yourself, do you know? How did they become a single parent?

2. Draw up a list of all the advantages and disadvantages of being on your own with the children.

3. Draw up a checklist of all the experiences you have faced since becoming a single parent and the things you would like to resolve.

2
What Kind of Parent Am I?

'There are 1.4 million single parents in the UK and they cover a wide spectrum from royalty to single parent dads living on a council estate. What people forget is that single parents are just ordinary parents who do not have the benefit of the other parent under the same roof.'

The title of this chapter is a very important question as it helps you to identify role models and support networks that will assist you in your aim of being not only a successful and confident parent but also a more fulfilled individual. The route to your single parenthood gives certain clues, for instance, a bereaved lone parent as opposed to a divorced mum, but there are also characteristics defined by age, gender, sexuality, disability, and relationship status. All single parents have common needs, but who you are and your experience define how you in turn define the role of parent.

There are many definitions of parenthood. The society you live in, the church, your parents and friends all have a view. However, *you* are your children's parent and you need to have a clear idea of how you define the role.

Is being a parent a job?
Yes, it is. It is not a job that you apply for in the normal way, and often it is not recognised as such. However, being a parent is very important and the skills you acquire are far ranging.

UNDERSTANDING THE JOB OF BEING A PARENT

The first step to understanding the job of parenting is to ask what are the accepted aims in the society we live in, as regards children. If you look around the world, whatever the culture, the general aims of being a parent are the same, although details vary. Education, for example, may be defined differently. It may mean teaching children to read and write or it may mean teaching children to tend sheep or fetch water.

Look at the box below which lists the things you do every day as a parent. You may have different words but the path is the same whatever your background. You may have particular views about method, because of social and cultural upbringing, but the overall aim is simply **to bring your children up to be healthy and happy individuals.**

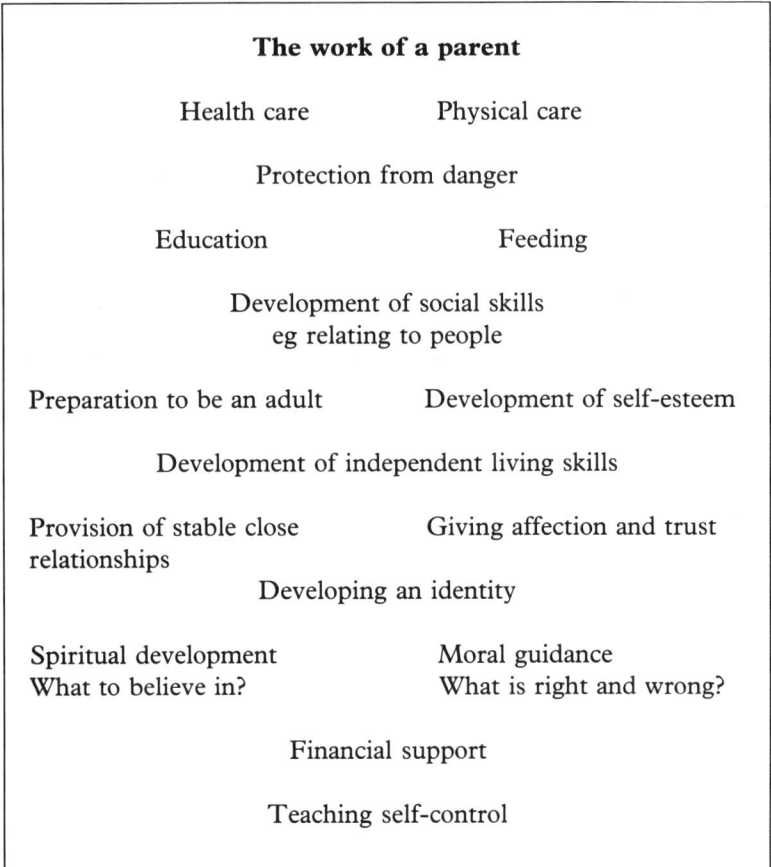

The work of a parent

Health care   Physical care

Protection from danger

Education   Feeding

Development of social skills
eg relating to people

Preparation to be an adult   Development of self-esteem

Development of independent living skills

Provision of stable close   Giving affection and trust
relationships
Developing an identity

Spiritual development   Moral guidance
What to believe in?   What is right and wrong?

Financial support

Teaching self-control

SEEING THE ROLE OF PARENT IN CONTEXT

It is important to remember that, even if you are a single parent, you are not on your own in your job of looking after your children. Fig. 1 shows some of the many other individuals, groups and institutions which have an influence on your child.

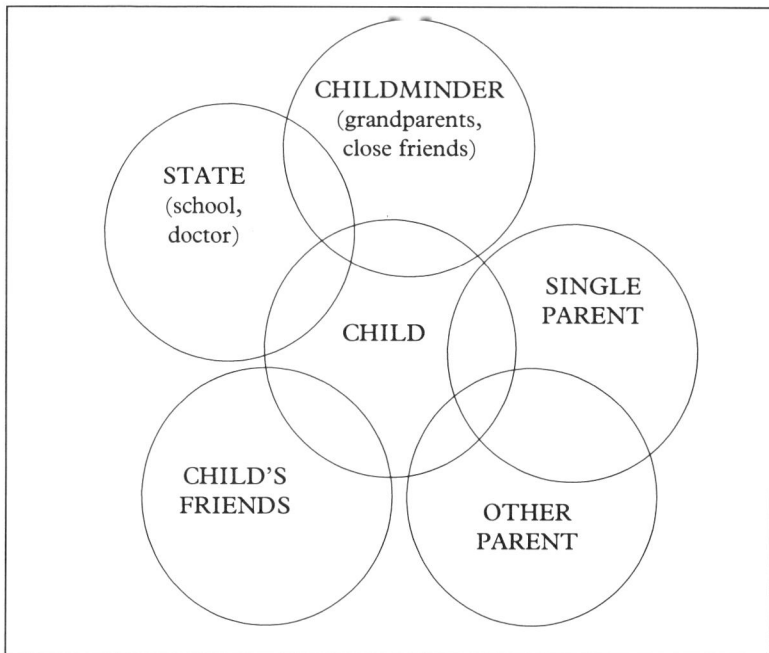

Fig. 1. The main influences on your child.

WHAT ARE MY RESPONSIBILITIES AS A PARENT?

The word 'responsibility' haunts every single parent, and the fact is that the parent who is left with the children after a relationship break-up, or a decision to keep a child after accidentally becoming pregnant, is the parent who fully accepts the day-to-day responsibility for the child.

'Parental responsibility' is a new concept introduced by the Children Act 1989, where it is defined as: '**All the rights, duties, powers, responsibilities and authority which by law a parent of a child has in relation to the child and his property**.'

What does this mean in practice? Here is a list of some of the rights and duties a single parent has:

● to name your child

● to protect and maintain your child

● to see your child attends school between 5 and 16 years old

- to choose your child's schooling

- to ensure your child receives medical treatment

- to appoint a guardian to look after your child in the event of your death

- to consent to your child's marriage if he/she is aged under 18

- to represent your child

- to decide where your child is to live

- to choose your child's religion

- to discipline your child.

Who has legal parental responsibility for my child?
Mothers and married fathers automatically have legal responsibility for their children. In the event of divorce, the courts have to decide on the rights of each parent. Unmarried fathers do not have any legal rights over their children unless they go to court and obtain a parental responsibility order or acquire custody. However, married or un-married fathers have a duty to maintain their children.

WRITING YOUR OWN PARENT'S JOB DESCRIPTION

Writing a description of your job as a parent will enable you to get a clear idea of how you see your role and what you feel should be the role of others (your ex-partner, the school, etc), as well as giving you the sense that you are doing an extremely important job.

Job title: Parent.

Main duties: A list of duties can be compiled by looking around you, at other parents, and by making a list of the things you do daily. For example, you take care of your children's health, talk to the doctor. You supervise your child's education by taking him/her to school, helping with homework, meeting your child's teacher.

Most awkward duties: What is the hardest thing you have to do?

Is it simply mending a bike, or the really difficult job of combining work with raising your child?

Most disagreeable duties: What do you hate doing? It could be meeting your ex-partner when he/she picks up the children.

Special features of the job: Your child may have a range of special needs that you have to acquire skills for: he/she may have learning difficulties, or be over active.

How do I know if I am doing OK as a parent? Only you can answer this question, but why not ask people around you?

EXPLORING THE DIFFERENT ROLE MODELS

Often the hard part of being a single parent is the isolation. You feel you are surrounded by other parents who are in happy relationships, 2.2 child families, although the fact is that society is changing and you are one of many in the same position. However, single parents often feel isolated even amongst other single parents. If you are a divorced mum, aged 38, with two children, you may feel isolated if you go along to a single parent club that is full of teenage mums. You may be a single parent father who feels lost amongst a group of divorced mums. It is important to identify that there is someone who has very similar experiences to you, and who can provide useful guides. For example, if you are a teenage mum fearful of your future with your new baby, it will help to meet another who has not only managed to bring up their child to be a healthy individual but also developed themselves, perhaps by going to college.

Parenting after marriage

The majority of single parents are women who have been in marriages that have ended for a variety of reasons, including separation, divorce or being widowed.

Case studies: Pam and Sue pick up the pieces

Pamela Davis's husband died suddenly and she was thrown into the role of being a single parent literally overnight: 'I never ever dreamt that my husband would die and that I would be on my own. It never entered my head. I was very happy. Suddenly I was on my own. I became a single parent. My world was shattered and in fact if the children had not been there I would have just ended my life. But I had two children to look after and had to go on. The everyday things of having to take them to school, get to work, wash clothes, make meals, meant I could keep going with half my brain switched off. It was late at night alone in bed that I felt the real impact of being alone. I was often relieved when the children crept into my bed for a cuddle. My attitude as a parent has not changed accept that now I have to do things my husband would have normally done. Now I can mend a bike and play a mean game of football.'

Sue Chan has experienced divorce twice but each time went into the relationship on the assumption that it was for ever: 'Perhaps I am just unlucky in love. My first marriage was when I was very young and I did not know what I was doing. But the second time I took a lot of time over my decision. I took advice. It still went wrong. No one wants their relationship to end, but no one wants to be hit by a violent husband or wants them to sleep with someone else. Perhaps years ago, women tolerated that behaviour. We don't have to now. I believe there are more divorces because women are standing up for their rights, which their mothers did not have.'

Breaking up outside marriage

There is no reason to expect relationships outside marriage to survive better than those within marriages. And a parent is a parent whatever the relationship with the partner.

Case study: Sally learns to do everything

Sally Hunt is classed as an unmarried mum, but lived with her ex-boyfriend for four years before she became pregnant. It was the pregnancy that destroyed the relationship: 'Brian just couldn't cope with the thought of the responsibility of being a parent. He went to stay with his parents and didn't come back. He came back for a short time but after Adam was born, he left. I started my life as a parent alone, I never shared the role, so my experience is that I have to do everything. Brian does not visit Adam, so Adam has no way of comparing parents. To him Mums do everything.'

Being a single parent dad

Men are very able to bring up their children alone, and 10 per cent of all single parent families are headed by a man.

Men tend to become lone parents when there is no other choice available to the children, ie their mother dies, leaves home or becomes severely incapacitated through illness or disability. However, more men are actively contesting the custody of their children and the courts are not automatically awarding custody to the mother as in the past. With the greater emphasis on conciliation and taking the fault aspects out of divorce, it is likely that more children will come under the immediate care of their father. There is a strong development in the concept of shared parenting where the child spends half the time with the father and half with the mother.

Case study: Martin changes his views on roles

Martin Lewis is bringing up his three children alone, after his wife left due to post-natal depression. He never imagined he was going to be a single parent: 'The whole system works on the basis that children should be with the mother. My immediate thoughts were that for men to be at home caring for the children is not natural. Men should be out in the world of work, creating role models for their children of what it is to be male. However, men as well as women *can* take care of children. Lone fathers are pioneers, opening up the boundaries around the question of who can do childcare. I firmly believe men and women's roles are interchangeable and men are as capable as women of nurturing children. Lone fathers resemble mothers more than they differ from them. We may have different styles of parenting to women but these need not be better or worse.'

Becoming a teenage mum

A teenage mum is the most vulnerable of all lone parents. Bringing up a child in any circumstances is a demanding job. Doing it alone is very hard. Doing it alone when very young is the hardest of all. Only 5 per cent of lone parents are teenage mums, and with improved contraceptive information, advice and support, the percentage is declining.

Many teenage mums get pregnant with the first boyfriend, often too shy to go to their doctors for contraception, or to talk to their boyfriends about it. They just thought it would never happen to them. This left them finding out they were pregnant and feeling scared, isolated, and unaware of the options open to them. Many teenage pregnancies are not discovered until the pregnancy is advanced. Often teenagers themselves have either not wanted to face the truth or genuinely been ignorant. They may have known but been scared to tell anyone.

Case study: Lucy becomes a teenage mum

Sue Chan's daughter Lucy became pregnant at 16: 'I left school in May and fell pregnant in October. I left school at 16, to live with my boyfriend. The relationship ended and at 18 I found myself as a single parent with a young child, and no permanent place to live. I moved back home with my mum. At school we didn't get proper sex education, so I didn't know where to go for contraception. I didn't pay attention at school, but I'm working hard at my education now because I want to become a teacher. When Daniel is at school I'll go to college. I'm doing my basic training now so I'm ready for it then. It's really hard being a single parent. I didn't really know what I was getting into when I was younger, but I'm looking forward to the future and I am determined to get on.'

Being a gay lone parent

Society is opening up, too fast or too slow, depending on your own personal view, and one of the taboos that is being broken is being gay and being a parent. Being a good parent is nothing to do with your sexuality. However, we live in a society that still tends to think of the 'norm' as children being cared for by a married couple (man and woman). So as a gay lone parent you are breaking two taboos at once.

What will happen to my children if I leave a relationship because I have discovered I am a lesbian?
The law has some way to go in catching up with changing lifestyles, and your ex-partner can state lesbian conduct as unreasonable behaviour in order for the divorce to go through. This could cause you problems if your partner decides to contest custody of the children.

Will my sexuality effect the development of my children?
Research into gay parenting shows few differences between children brought up by gay and lesbian parents and their heterosexually reared schoolmates. It is important for children to know their parents are happy and relatively stress free which is hard to achieve if you are under stress from a marriage break-up or you are coming to terms with your sexuality.

While it is preferable that parents place a high priority on their children's needs, this must not exclude considering your own needs for personal fulfilment in whatever sort of adult relationship you desire. Common sense suggests that people who are contented in themselves are more likely to be able to be generous and supportive parents.

DISCUSSION POINTS

1. Find out if there are any single parent support groups in your area. Ask at the library or at your Citizens' Advice Bureau.

2. Write your own job description. List all the things you have to do as a parent.

3. List all the things that you do now, but had never thought you would do before becoming a lone parent.

3
Facing the Realities of Splitting Up

'Every relationship is unique. It is special and that makes any split-up traumatic. It can also be a relief if there have been long periods of violence and tension. Although the reasons for splitting up are wide ranging, violence and infidelity are the common stated reasons. It is important to remember that our divorce laws have been based on the principle of finding fault. In reality, most of us are basically disillusioned with our partner, or they with us.'

The process of splitting up involves an erosion of the relationship, which can include long periods of silence, angry and violent arguments, and deep distrust. In some cases, one partner believes everything is OK until the other declares they have been having an affair and are going to leave. It is quite common for men to leave, to live with the other woman, just after their wife/girlfriend has given birth.

Money plays a major part today in the collapse of relationships. Loss of work, high debts, and repossession of the home all cause stress and erode the very foundations of the relationship. This book is not concerned with the rights and wrongs of splitting up, and does not seek to put blame on any parties. It is purely a practical guide to facing up to the realities and you need to take a deep breath and face them too.

WHAT HAPPENS WHEN A COUPLE SPLIT UP

Most of us can remember the actual day of the split in every detail. We may be very cloudy about the events leading up to it, as often it is a slow build up, but the day itself is vivid. The day the straw broke the camel's back.

Your relationship was about two people making a formal or informal contract to live together, buy property together, socialise together, and have children together. When it ends, you need to untie the knots. This includes deciding who the children will live with, dividing property, one partner moving out, loss of two incomes or your sole income if you are a full-time house parent, separating your names from all documentation (bank accounts, gas bills etc), and telling family and friends that you are not a twosome anymore. You become single again but with the added advantage of having the companionship of your child or children.

I have been married for ten years and now we're splitting up. What do I do?
The untying of the relationship knot can be a painful, confusing, time-consuming and generally unhappy period. There are a number of choices open to you. You may wish to go ahead with a full divorce or prefer to opt for the interim steps of separation. Divorce is a legal process which includes resolving what should happen with the children, housing and maintenance. You have three main routes to start the process:

1. Talk things out with your ex-partner and come to a friendly and mutual agreement.

2. Use a conciliation and mediation service or a counselling service such as Relate.

3. Use a solicitor.

It is important that you seek proper advice, as the consequences could be with you a long time.

I am not married but lived with my partner for three years. What happens when we split up?
If you have not been married to your partner there is no legal procedure to go through when splitting up. In some circumstances you or your partner may decide that you want to go to court to establish rights to housing or with regard to the children. Child maintenance is liable from the other parent whether you are married or not. However, maintenance for you is only available if you have been married. Important points to consider when splitting up include:

- arrangements for contact with your children

- money for yourself and your children

- housing

- any cohabitation agreement that you may have had

- a will—remember to think about what happens to your children if you die tomorrow. Frightening but you need to be practical at this time.

UNDERSTANDING YOUR FEELINGS

Breaking up from your partner is never an easy thing to do, especially if you have children. Your head is swimming with feelings and emotions, pain, grief and anger, and yet there are also all the practical things you have to sort out:

Where will I live?
How will we split up the house?
What are we going to live on?
Are the children going to see the other parent?

You are frightened and confused. Everything is complicated and all you want to do is crawl into bed and hide.

There is a terrifying sense of unreality about what is happening to you. A relationship has died and you need to grieve. It will help to talk to a close friend or relative, or even seek a professional counsellor, or go to a single parent support group. This will enable you to start to come to terms with your feelings and realise you are not alone. Your feelings are natural and understanding them is part of the healing process.

Will I survive all this?
Yes, you will. It is interesting to note that the research has shown that people with children survive better the traumas of splitting up and divorce, because of the simple fact of having the children. You have to get up every morning and feed the kids, get them to school. You have to keep going.

USING CONCILIATION AND MEDIATION

Conciliation and mediation are terms used to refer to ways of coming to an agreement with your ex-partner about the arrangements of splitting up. The hope is that an independent mediator will take some of the emotion out of the situation and enable you to get down to practicalities.

Mediation is done by discussion and negotiation and is available to married and unmarried couples. One or two trained workers sit with you and try to help you keep the discussion to practical issues. Priority is given to the welfare of the children, but some services also help with financial negotiations.

Using mediation can be far better than trying to resolve issues through the courts. It is also cheaper as the service is usually charged by the hour and most mediation services work out their fee according to your ability to pay.

Can I use this service without the co-operation of my ex?
Yes. You go along and talk over the issues that need to be resolved. The service will write to your partner and ask them to come and initially talk to them on their own. When they have an agreement to co-operate with the process, they will bring both parties together.

How do I find a conciliation service?
There are services all round the country, and following revision of the divorce laws, new services are planned. Your solicitor, local County Court and Citizens' Advice Bureau will have details. The main national mediation services are listed at the back of this book.

SORTING OUT YOUR LIFE ALONE

You have split up from your partner, and you are alone with your children. This is the reality. Perhaps you started out with a plan to be with a partner and have children. You now have the children but the partner has gone. Your life is going to change dramatically.

You need to divide your thinking and planning into two sections, one that deals with the immediate short-term goals and another that looks at the long term. Your short-term aim is to make sure you have a roof over you and your child's head, money to live on, food in your belly, and enough time to slowly heal the wounds. The long-term aim is to find peace of mind and happiness (whatever that may mean for you) for yourself and your children. You must believe that it is possible as it is only you who can achieve this aim.

There is going to be a complete cultural change. There is only one of you and you have to take over full responsibility for the children. This may not be too big a change depending on how much parental support you had before. You will face the reality of being a lone parent the day you are ill and need to stay in bed, but have to find the energy at the bottom of your reserves to get up and feed your kids breakfast.

The important key to coping with a split-up and the first steps of lone parenthood is to try and keep the existing routines in regard to the children and take things day by day.

Anyone who has experienced a family split-up will readily admit to the pure pain and the complexity of untying the knots—including joint accounts, shared income, the home. Concentrate on the practicalities, by listing the priorities.

Priority one

This heading should cover issues which, if not sorted out immediately, could put you and your children in danger. For example:

Issue	Problem	Questions	Action
Housing:	*Is my house safe?*	If it is a council house, or private rented accommodation, is it in my name?	Visit the Council's Housing Advice Centre or the Citizens' Advice Bureau
		If it is mortgaged, are the payments going to be made? Is it in my name?	Get advice, speak to the Building Society.
		I know I am going to be homeless. How am I going to get a home?	Speak to the Council's Housing Advice Centre or the Citizens' Advice Bureau.
My children:	*The other parent*	How do I get maintenance?	Speak to your solicitor, the Citizens' Advise Bureau, the Child Support Agency.

Finish the questions below by working out what your action should be:

My children:	*Childcare*	How are my children cared for when I am at work or at college?	
Money:	*How do I live?*	I cannot keep my job up and need to look after my children full-time. How are we to live? What money will come in?	
		I owe money which I cannot pay. What shall I do?	

My husband fully supported us and what do I do without his money coming in?

Work: *Can I keep my job?* The hours are not compatible with picking up the children. What shall I do?

Priority two

This heading covers issues that are not life and death questions but are nevertheless important and need resolving eventually. They may be very simple things and/or longer-term self-fulfilment ones. Ask the children to contribute to this list as it will help you see how their priorities fit in with yours.

What do I need to do to get my life sorted out?

You need to make sure that:

- all the legal formalities are undertaken and you and your children clearly know your position in regard to the other parent;

- your housing is safe;

- all official bodies know you have separated and all relevant accounts are solely in your name. Beware of joint bank accounts and credit cards. You don't want your partner to run up unnecessary bills.

Checklist of who to inform about the split

- landlord, housing office or mortgage lender

- council tax office and Inland Revenue

- DSS and housing benefit office

- water company

- gas and electricity companies

- your child's school, so that the school can help if the child seems upset

- the bank, if you have a joint account and want to close it

- hire purchase or credit companies, with a proposal for how the debt is to be repaid

- insurance companies, if you have a joint policy

- telephone company

- the Post Office if you need your mail redirecting

- the doctor, dentist and/or child health clinic.

GETTING SUPPORT AND ADVICE

'I had no one to turn to, to talk to, to get help and support. I was alone, constantly asked by my children what I was going to do. I didn't know. So many things had to be done, but I did not even have the energy to ask for help. In fact I did not know where to go. When people asked me whether I wanted help, I was too shy to answer yes, but said I was OK, when I wasn't.'

Loneliness, isolation and sheer lack of energy is a common state for many single parents and it is often seen as more of a hurdle to get support than it is to try and solve your problems on your own. You will be very surprised how relieved you feel when you make the first steps of talking things through with people who are having the same experience or are expert in the many issues that affect you every day.

What help do I need?
You need both practical help and emotional support. Practical help includes advice on the legal and technical process of separating, sorting out financial matters and finding somewhere to live, but also domestic issues like babysitting, childcare, mending the bike, or even shopping. Emotional support may mean a shoulder to cry on, a sympathetic ear, looking after the children when you have to go out to see your solicitor or enquire about benefits, or going out for the evening to learn what it is to have fun again.

Who can I turn to for help and support?
There are many people and organisations out there who can help you. It is a question of finding the right one. They include family/relatives, friends, other parents, your children's teachers, people at your local

church/temple/synagogue, neighbours, the local council (housing department), Citizens' Advice Bureau, local community worker, lone parent group, solicitor, mediation service. Your local library is often a good place to start as they should have a list of local support agencies and groups.

When do I need help from others?
You are not superhuman. You may need help when you cannot cope physically because of illness, or when you simply do not understand that threatening letter you have just received.

I find it hard to ask for help. I don't want people to think I am unable to cope.
Do not be afraid to ask. It is a strength not a weakness. Many professional services are there to help. It is their job. If people did not use the services they would be out of a job. Asking for help is a positive part of self-help. You are not asking someone to do things for you, you are asking for practical advice on solving your problems. Just remember all the times you have helped others, and all the people you will help in the future.

Make a list of all your supporters and the organisations that could help you. Use the following examples to get you thinking.

Help I need?	*Who gives it now?*	*Who could give it?*
finding a new home	my dad	local council
sort out my money problems	no one	Citizens' Advice Bureau
my ex-partner is calling around unannounced	next door neighbour	solicitor, police, mediation service

HELPING YOUR CHILDREN UNDERSTAND

'They did miss their dad. I couldn't really cope with it. I just shut off.'

You will find it difficult and painful to cope with the breakdown of a relationship, and it can be easy at this time to overlook or misunderstand your children's needs and feelings. If you are a single parent through a relationship ending you will realise that splitting up is not one single event which is over and done with in a week, a month or a year. It causes changes which continue for a long time, but this can be to your advantage as it can be used to help your children understand and adapt to differences in their lives. You and your children need to find out how daily life and relationships can be rearranged to suit your particular circumstances.

Children rarely want their parents to separate and will go to incredible lengths to try to keep you together. They are used to the problems that cause the separation and even get used to parents storming out and not returning for several weeks as long as they do come back! The point when a couple decide to separate can be confusing for all children. They seldom take part in the decision and yet they are profoundly affected by it. Children often talk of feeling like an outsider and being ignored whilst adults try to sort themselves out. They describe how they are left to worry about what will happen to them and how lonely they can feel. Children want you to be honest with them even if they don't fully understand. Often children talk of being afraid that their parents will stop loving them like they stopped loving each other. Most children wonder if they are somehow to blame for the situation and are filled with guilt and regret for all the times when they have been naughty.

The child's reaction

The range of emotions a child experiences depends largely on the circumstances surrounding the separation. Each child will react differently, but there are some general trends. Most children suddenly realise that their parents are not perfect and respect their parents less as a result. Many experience shock, either as numbness so they seem not to be affected at all, or they begin to catch every cough and cold around. Denial is common as it the feeling of betrayal, which can often lead to anger and aggression. The most destructive emotion of all is hate as it can affect a child's future relationships and cause lasting damage to their ability to function as a balanced and relaxed person.

There is a marked difference between the ways different age groups react:

3- to 5-year-olds struggle to explain how they feel and seem bewildered. Many regress and return to familiar habits of thumb-sucking or clingy behaviour as a way of recapturing the security of the past. They need help to understand what has happened and reassurance that it is not their fault. They need to know about practicalities like who will look after the cat and if they can take toys with them.

6- to 8-year-olds usually express real grief, crying, sobbing and sometimes even searching for the lost parent. Often their behaviour in school deteriorates. At this age, boys are particularly vulnerable and need a lot of reassurance.

9- to 12-year-olds can appear very angry and hostile, looking for someone or something to blame. They may even suffer from psychosomatic illnesses, sometimes unconsciously hoping that their illness will bring their parents back together again. Often there will be concerns from the school that the child's work and attitude are poor.

Teenagers often try to hide their mental bewilderment behind a complete refusal to see or talk to one parent. They can express their hurt through physical aggression or even vandalism as they try to distance themselves from their emotions and show an 'I don't care' attitude to their friends. Adolescents are sometimes so embarrassed that they pretend nothing has happened and even deny the separation if their friends ask about it. Truanting and general lack of co-operation can be a feature.

I feel so guilty when I think of the children
You shouldn't feel guilty for separating. You had your reasons, but remember that while you may feel you are doing what is best for your family, your children may not feel this at all. You need to listen to them as well as getting them to listen to you.

How will my children react with only one parent?
It is not being part of a one parent family that causes children distress, but the feelings they experience that come from having to put up with something they did not want to happen. It is important to separate the two so as not to fall into the trap of believing that children are 'deprived' because they are from lone parent families.

   Key points to remember include:

- Provide honest and accurate information to your children in ways they can understand.

- Talk openly with your children so that they can make sense of what is going on.

- Give children the chance to air their feelings and their worries about the present and the future.

- Keep the children as secure as possible and lives as unchanged as much as possible in other ways.

- Help your children keep their own identities by encouraging contact with their friends, relatives and others who care for them.

- Tell the children frequently that you love them.

- Do not let your bitterness or anger about your ex-partner affect your child's relationship with the absent parent.

Above all, don't be afraid to tell your children how you feel. Many adults find it difficult to talk about feelings to their children. You may be afraid that you will lose control and the children will see you in distress. Sometimes there is a fear of losing face. Adults are supposed to be strong and able to cope. Sometimes we want to protect our children from extreme emotions as these may be too painful.

COMING TO TERMS WITH THE OTHER PARENT

You will need to sort out a range of issues with your ex-partner, including maintenance, access to the children and the division of property. These will normally be handled through a solicitor, the Child Support Agency and the conciliation services. These issues are dealt with in other chapters.

Away from the formalities of splitting up and the emotional anguish, it is important to have the long-term aim of coming to terms with the other parent for the benefit of your children. If a child can continue to have a good relationship with both parents even though they no longer are a family they are much less affected by the separation. Any continuing conflict between parents increases the effects on the child. The most serious damage is usually done when a child no longer sees one parent at all.

It is an awful statistic to quote, but over 50 per cent of fathers of children now living solely with their mother have no contact at all. This is not healthy in the long term for children as they are conceived by two parents and they may have had some of their most formative years with two parents under the same roof.

Your children need to feel they have the freedom to keep in contact. We are extensions of our parents and our identity comes from them. Our own development needs to establish these links. It is not easy and in some cases not advisable, eg if there has been a history of violence, but if it can be achieved, you will find it beneficial for your children.

DISCUSSION POINTS

1. Make a list of every person and every organisation that needs to be informed of your new situation. Check who has been informed.

2. Draw up a priority one and priority two list of what needs sorting out.

3. Find out if there is a local conciliation/mediation service in your area.

4
What to do After the Death of a Partner

'I defy anyone to say that bereavement is not the worst trauma of all. In split-up situations, however much one partner may hate what the other has done, at least that person is alive. If they have to be contacted, even if that is unpleasant, they usually can be by way of telephone, letter or through solicitors. But neither the cleverest of lawyers not the most splendid of magicians can convey a message to a partner who has died. Whatever the misery caused to children by separation, nothing can compensate a child for the despairing loss of a parent by death. At least a live parent can be contacted by the child at some point in their lives. For the bereaved child that "goodbye" is for ever.'

The trouble is—you don't know what to do. Death has probably never come so close. It is a new experience and you don't know how to deal with it. This chapter can describe ways of coping but in the end it is up to you. Whether death is sudden or expected, it is always a shock. You have children and never wanted or expected to be on your own. You have been made a single parent through no fault of your own, nature has dealt a cruel blow. You are once again a single person, older and with kids in tow, your relationship has ended and you have to start a new life.

There is not space here to cover the immediate practical issues of managing a death, such as arranging a funeral etc. The sections on further reading and useful addresses should point you towards publications and organisations that will be better placed to help you with those aspects. This chapter concentrates on what it means for you to become a single parent through bereavement.

FACING THE BEWILDERMENT

No one who has not experienced the death of a partner can fully understand all its conflicting emotions. Some say it is like becoming a teenager again with all a teenager's swings of mood. You can become over sensitive to casual remarks, dread waking up in the morning, that's if you are sleeping at all. Waking up at weekends can be a nightmare. You may speak aloud to your ex-partner, and your mind will drift to happy times. All these feelings are normal and there is no right way to grieve. The 'grieving timetable' below shows a common pattern, but it is important to remember that the stages often overlap, and that every person's experience is different. You have to find a way through by whatever methods bring most relief and comfort. Usually becoming a single parent through death brings a wide range of support from family friends, teachers, everyone who knows you. Many will give advice, but in the end you have to fight your way through.

Grieving timetable

1. Shock
2. Numbness
3. Struggle between fantasy and reality
4. Feeling of guilt and frenzy
5. Depression
6. Release through crying
7. Painful memories
8. Acceptance

Case study: Pamela copes with sudden death

Pamela Davis's husband died suddenly at 30, and left her to bring up her two sons alone. She remembers her first experiences vividly.

' "Will we have to give up football mummy?" How do you answer a question like that from a little lad of seven whose dad has just died? That was my son's reaction. I reacted by putting the dustbin out and feeding the dog. Realisation was yet to dawn.

It was in the early hours one hot, sunny morning when I woke to find my husband dead in bed beside me. I could not accept what was happening. I was perfectly calm. Having phoned the doctor, I phoned again to apologise for disturbing them with such awful lies. My husband wasn't dead, just over tired. It was early Monday morning and we'd had a very hectic weekend.

Fortunately, our doctor was already knocking on my door as I put the phone down, though I was still convinced we didn't need a visit. David and I had argued about the choice of carpet and I remember thinking when I took the doctor into the bedroom that it was a good job he wasn't dead as I'd have wanted him to have his choice of carpet if time was so short.

The doctor carried out her examination and then gently led me downstairs, put the kettle on, sat me down and told me David was dead and as far as she could tell had been for about four hours. He'd had a massive heart attack—he was 30.

My first reaction was that I must get the children up as they would be late for school. It sounds unbelievable but they had not woken up through all this. I started to hear the children stir upstairs. From the unnatural silence which followed being told my husband was dead, I started hearing things being dropped, the loo flushing. Still, I was numb, rather like coming round from an anaesthetic, completely relaxed and detached from the situation. I did get the children to school and to the childminder. They were told daddy was unwell and amazingly they accepted that and instead asked questions about packed lunches and football shirts. Finally, as they left with my next door neighbour, I started to feel cold and to shiver. I tried to put the gas fire on but it was broken. Now the tears came and there was no stopping them. I sobbed for a long time and it was the fact that the gas fire wouldn't work that triggered me off. The doctor said to me people either sink or swim and somehow she knew I'd swim. My son hasn't given up football.'

SHARING THE GRIEF WITH YOUR CHILDREN

You must follow your own instinct in handling your children after the death of your partner. It is a good idea not to shut children out of your grief. It is impossible to protect them completely from what has happened, but you must feel assured that they will get over it and not suffer permanent emotional damage.

There is a tendency to tell little lies initially about the death. Children are told daddy is ill in hospital or has gone away. But if you don't fully tell them, eventually they will find out. Honesty is the best way.

As well as the shock and disbelief at the death of a parent, a child may be afraid of losing the other parent as well. It is important to allow your child to talk about his/her fears.

Asking questions
● How are the children coping?

● Would they benefit from talking to a counsellor?

- Are your children's friends still coming round to play?

- Do you talk about their deceased parent?

Taking action
- Why not encourage them to make a special scrapbook about their parent by using photographs and pictures?

- Talk about how their parent had loved them, how you love them.

- Discuss with them what their parent would have wanted for them.

- Tell them what hopes you have for them.

- Share your hopes for the future and make plans with them.

- Be open and honest. Talk about finances and what you need to do now in building up a new life. Involve them and you will be surprised how resourceful and helpful they can be.

FINDING THE RIGHT SUPPORT

Often there is plenty of support at the time of death but this can evaporate as time goes on and you may well find yourself needing more support than you are getting from friends and family during the two years after a partner's death. Sources of support include parents, children, friends, support groups, professional caregivers and counsellors.

What makes a good listener?
A good listener should be non-judgmental, accepting, able to hear the bad as well as the good and not afraid of anger.

Who do I talk to?
Your local branch of the Citizens' Advice Bureau can supply details of bereavement services and counsellors in your area. Your GP can also make referrals to counsellors or therapists. Even if they are not what you want they can be a good starting point.

Case study: Pamela experiences grief and healing
Pamela was advised by her doctor to go to a bereavement counsellor: 'The best help I found early on was the visit from a bereavement counsellor. The visits lasted about nine months. I found it easier to

talk to a stranger, although that stranger became a good friend. I was able to let off steam, be angry, cry, be miserable, feel guilty and even laugh. Yes, even laugh. At first I felt as if I was betraying David. At times I also felt very angry at him for leaving me and the boys. The counsellor was very helpful in pointing out that all these emotions were normal. It is OK to be angry. It is OK to laugh. As the days went by the happy times outweighed the sad times. It is all part of the healing process.'

DISCUSSION POINTS

1. Look at the grieving timetable on page 45 and work out what stage you feel you are at.

2. Contact and investigate all your local support groups and find one that fits your needs.

3. Work with your children on making up a special scrapbook.

5
Bringing Up Your Children on Your Own

'Being a parent is exhausting enough in a family that has the benefit of two parents involved in the day-to-day care of children, but on your own it can be a real uphill struggle as the buck stops with you. This can be an advantage as you often don't have to consult the absent parent, and get into unnecessary disagreements. However, doing everything, often without anyone giving a helping hand or giving you an occasional lie-in, can be very tiring and lonely. This means that the real bond is with your children, and it is their love which is so important, which keeps you going.'

You may have started your single parenthood from day one of your child's birth and therefore have the benefit of planning your life around the fact that you are the sole everyday parent. However, the majority of single parents have had a period of time bringing up their children in a two parent family. The definition of what the two parent family entails is very wide, and over the last 50 years the roles of men and women in the family gave have changed radically. Bringing up your children on your own is simply defined as doing practically everything, and if society defines by the law of nature that you need two parents to bring up a child effectively, 'on your own' means that you have to be prepared to do two jobs in the home, and possibly three if you go out to work. In fact many single parents have to do a number of jobs in order to carry out their home role, as they cannot fit a full-time job around the care hours. It is very hard work and should not be underestimated.

The key is to see the family as a whole unit. In fact, you are not on your own, but live with your children, and as a family you develop with each other. You are the parent and in control, but your children are partners and helpers. You are on a road of adventure together. It isn't them against you.

LOOKING POSITIVELY AT THE BENEFITS

Being the number one parent has many disadvantages but also many benefits and the biggest benefit is your children. You have created these wonderful, at times annoying, individuals who have the ability to make you laugh and cry in a matter of seconds. On an everyday basis you call the tune—you do not have to cope with adult arguments, threatened or actual violence, and picking up the pieces of the adult child, your ex-partner. You may at times, late at night, cry out for adult company, but you will never be alone, because when you do cry, you will be surprised when a little hand will reach out to touch you.

What is it like to be a child? How do your children see you?
To understand the benefits of bringing up your children alone, you need to understand them a bit better. Start enjoying them and see them as good fun rather than a trap or a noose around your neck. Try and remember how you felt when you were a child. How would you have liked your parents to bring you up? Then consider what it is like to be your children. What is it like for them to have you as a parent?

What do you want your children to grow up like?
Life as a single parent often seems to involve only the day-to-day survival business, of washing, cleaning, getting them to school, cooking, feeding, mending, shopping. It is easy to lose sight of what you want for them in the future, as well as understanding what they want.

BALANCING YOUR CHILDREN'S AND YOUR NEEDS

You are important and your needs are just as essential as your children's. You need to make time for yourself and get your children to take more responsibility for themselves. New-born babies can do nothing for themselves. They depend on you totally for survival. They cry, you comfort them; when they are hungry, you feed them; when they are dirty, you change their nappies. However, as children grow, they become more capable of leading their own lives, and meeting their own needs. It may be only holding their cup or crawling to get a toy, or eventually walking to school on their own. They are making decisions all the time.

Case study: Sue feels lonely

Sue Chan suffered very bad bouts of depression, as she was doing everything for her children, and had little time for herself: 'I was feeling alone the other night. We were all sitting watching television and I felt terribly alone and then I looked around me and saw my children and realised I wasn't. I realised that I needed to make sure that my life had a balance of adult company, and that was for me to sort out.'

What am I doing for me?

Write down your ten favourite activities, things you really like to do just for yourself and would do even, or perhaps especially, if you didn't have kids. Then make a list of how often you now do each activity, as in the box below.

Activity	**I do this:**				
	Often	Sometimes	Hardly ever	Never	I would like to do this more
Going for a walk					
Going to the cinema					
Reading a book					
Going dancing					
Having sex					

The point of this exercise is to reaffirm that you have needs and need the time to fulfil them. Now think how you will make this list possible.

Everyone has needs and children can be very clever in getting them

Needs	How does your child get it?	How do you?
For attention		
To feel fully part of the family		
To develop own sense of independence		
For security		
To explore and learn		
To feel useful		

met. Think of how your child gets his/her needs fulfilled and how you do. Use the box above to get you thinking.

Key points

● New-born babies depend on you to meet all their needs. Older children do not.

● Your role as parent changes over time.

● Handing over responsibility for doing things provides valuable practice for life.

● Looking after your needs teaches a child to be more receptive to their own.

● Taking care of yourself and getting what you want gives a good example to your children.

● If you get too good at looking after your children's needs and solving their problems, you prevent them solving their problems themselves.

● When your children are arguing you do not have to get involved.

NEGOTIATING WITH THE OTHER PARENT

This is a very tricky subject and when you have been through a traumatic and bitter split-up, the mere thought of seeing your ex-partner is enough to drive you into a sweat. You have to decide what is best for your child. But don't forget they have views, and even a child who has never seen their other parent one day asks the fatal question, where is my daddy/mummy?

Usually the children have not been part of the decision to become part of a single parent family. Even if they have benefitted from it, you need to understand their needs in wanting to have contact with their other parent and to feel loved by that parent. Eventually it is preferable that you are able to establish a bitterness-free zone, and a way that the children can benefit from access to the other parent.

Case study: Sue's ex maintains contact

Sue Chan's first marriage ended after years of violence and her first husband has little contact with her and her oldest daughter, from that marriage. However, her second husband has regular contact with his children and the older daughter, whom he sees as very much his own.

'I regularly talk to Michael about the kids and he comes with me to school functions. My eldest daughter suffered from lack of contact with her real dad, as he was kind to her and never violent as he was to me. She has spent a lot of time trying to keep contact with him and for many years blamed me. When my second marriage broke down I did not want the same thing to happen again especially as my two youngest were still toddlers. Their father loves them and my eldest, Lucy, very much. Even though the divorce was painful, the memories of my daughter's experience made me make a special effort to make sure that the children had good contact with their dad.'

UNDERSTANDING THE EMOTIONAL EFFECTS

There are two main emotional events on the road to single parenthood; first the splitting up from or death of a partner and second the simple reality of being alone with your children. Every situation is different and each of us will feel a range of emotions which can leave scars on you and your children if you let them.

You need to find a way of understanding your feelings, and that they are very natural. As the parent who is simply left behind, it is natural for you to take the whole world's problems on your shoulders and this can create an unseen black rain cloud to follow you around. You need to find ways of bringing the sun out, and pushing other people's problems back to them. The past is the past and whatever we do we cannot change it. Hindsight is a perfect science. We act as best as we can in any given situation and often on reflection afterwards we probably would have liked to do things differently. The 'what ifs' will always haunt us. You need to move forward and put the past firmly back in the cupboard, learn from past mistakes but not fret over them.

Case study: Martin struggles to cope

Martin Lewis's wife left him suddenly giving him little notice: 'One day I was part of a two parent, three-children family, and the next day one parent had gone. My wife just could not cope any more with bringing up three very young kids and me. She had very bad depression after Steven was born and this became worse after Mark. I tried to give support but I had a demanding job and was on a short-term contract and continually fearful I would lose my job. The fear of insecurity for my family kept me working long hours. I became blind to what was happening to my wife. Suddenly I was on my own and this devastated me. I just tried to keep going and as the children were young I initially kept working full time. I had little time to think. My ex-wife started visiting regularly and we built up a good friendship that benefited us and the children. At one of her visits, I finally broke down in tears. It had taken nearly eight years. I loved my wife so much that I never really understood what had happened. It was like someone dying, without telling you why. I felt so alone. I always protected my children and never showed any bitterness, and made sure the children had contact with their mum. I kept them happy. Years later, my daughter told a friend that as neither I nor her mum ever explained to her what had happened she felt guilty that it had been her fault. She blamed herself. She was only 5 when Amanda left. I always thought we had explained, obviously not.'

FACING THE PREJUDICES OF SOCIETY

'SINGLE PARENTS CRIPPLE LIVES'
(The Telegraph, 2 August 1991)

'We must face the truth about these tragic children. One parent families bring misery for parents, young people . . . and society.'
(Daily Mail, 2 August 1991)

The above headlines are some of the many that are seen by us and our children continually. They are hurtful, cruel, insensitive and in the main wrong. A former General Secretary of the Professional Association of Teachers told his annual conference that it was 'a matter of fact' that children from single parent families were more likely to do badly at school, more likely to be poorly fed and clothed, ill-treated at home, and to get into trouble with the law. This sort of statement is very common and causes lone parent families to carry a universal stigma around them. It is a statement that is wrong.

Some children are deprived and some children who are deprived come from single parent families. But that doesn't mean all single parent households produce deprived children. The tabloid press have a habit of taking a little information and drawing wider conclusions. One part of a council estate that has a number of teenage mums becomes a photo picture for the nation on single parent families. The reality is that every section of society has single parent families, from royalty to the very poorest.

Case study: Pamela feels stigmatised

Pamela Davis is a widow but she still faces prejudice as a lone parent.

'My husband died, I work and bring up three children on my own, but I'm stigmatised as a poor little single parent family screwing the state. Many of my friends are single parents and some are on state benefit, but they are doing all they can to bring up their children to be good individuals. The absence of affordable childcare and lack of flexible and well-paid employment condemns many single parents, women and men, to a lifetime of poverty. But I also know many women in relationships that have the same problems, so it is wrong to single out lone parents as somehow guilty of self-inflicted poverty. No one does that. A man losing a job can throw a whole family into a downwards spiral that means they fall into the poverty trap. It is the same when a family is left with one full-time caring parent. They are hit badly financially and this takes years to sort out. The welfare system was created to help people who fall into this situation. There should be a range of initiatives that allow them to fight back.'

CARING FOR CHILDREN WITH SPECIAL NEEDS

The term 'special needs' is very wide and can encompass down's syndrome to dyslexia, asthma to ataxia. One in five children have special needs and as there are 2.3 million children cared for by single parents in the UK, it is estimated that 440,000 of these children have a range of needs that require special support.

Bringing up children alone is hard enough but giving further time and support to a child with special needs is extremely hard. In many cases it means that 100 per cent of time has to be devoted to being a parent and you have to rely heavily on state benefits as there is little opportunity to undertake other work. You deserve a lot of praise as well as a lot of support. You've really got a lot to cope with. Don't be afraid or too proud to ask for help. There are people who can do a lot for you, but you've got to let them know you are there. A range of organisations which can help you are listed under Useful Addresses at the back of this book.

LINKING HOME AND SCHOOL LIFE

Children usually enjoy school and school is the second greatest influence on their lives. Children enjoy learning, doing, taking on challenges, having a sense of achievement. It is important for them to share these experiences with the adults who are important in their lives. This includes you, their other parent if around, and their teachers. It can also mean other relatives, grandparents, older brothers and sisters, youth workers. But the home-school link is of prime importance, and along with sharing the good news, children also want to share the bad news. A child's parents splitting up or a parent dying does have a traumatic effect on any child and the school will find out about it, whether you like it or not. In fact, they *should* know. Do not be afraid to tell them. The school is a service to you, and you have rights in choosing which school your child goes to, and whatever your circumstances a teacher has the responsibility of making sure your child enjoys school and achieves their full potential. You should see it as a partnership, and as in the case of any partnership you should inform the other of your change in circumstances so that the teacher can be supportive and understand your child more. Teachers in the main are experienced and the reality is that every school class in the UK has children that come from single parent households.

LEARNING TO HAVE FUN WITH YOUR CHILDREN

As a single parent you often have little time to think let alone having fun. You are doing all the domestic chores, taking the children back and forth to school, perhaps holding down a job. But you still need to laugh and have fun. Enjoy your children's company—it's amazing what good therapy they can be. It's not easy as you are continually engaged in battles, or the post arrives and you are faced with another problem, another bill that cannot be paid. The other chapters in this book suggest a range of ways to fight off your many problems, but you also need to let your hair down a bit and show your children that there are happy moments when life can in fact be fun.

Break the routine. Instead of going home straight after school, go to the park. Take some bread and feed the ducks. Or turn the television off and get the family around a table and play a game.

Make a list of all the things you like doing and all things your children like doing. Look at the things that you have in common. When was the last time you did them together?

LOOKING AT THE OPTION OF SHARED PARENTING

The old saying, 'two heads are better than one', can be true if the two heads, in this case the two parents, can break the ice and find a way of communicating in regard purely to the children. Remember the past is the past.

Shared parenting means that after divorce and separation, both mother and father retain a positive parenting role in their children's lives. Sometimes it is called joint physical or joint actual custody or the newer contept of shared parental responsibility. Shared parenting is simply where the children spend substantial amounts of time with both parents—anything from a 30/70 split upwards. It is different from the notion of reasonable access or contact. Normally one parent has full legal custody of the child, and the other has visiting rights. All decisions on the child are made by the main 'home based' parent. In shared parenting, the children will normally live with one parent but regularly visit and stay with the other and both parents discuss issues regarding the children. The clear advantages of this arrangement can be:

- **Financial**—the other parent will feel happy to target money to the children.

- **Support**—there is always the other parent, in the event of illness, for example.

- **Children**—the children feel at ease with both parents and this gives a sense of balance. They are also prevented from playing one off against the other.

Case study: Martin and Amanda learn to share the parenting

After some years Martin Lewis and his ex-wife have built up a stronger relationship that enables them to discuss their children more fully. Amanda has the children during holidays and occasionally comes over for weekends so that Martin can get away.

'It was hard at first as my wife left because of illness, and all I wanted was for her to come home. When she was better she wanted to divorce and this was a painful process. Three years later I was in a second relationship which also made it difficult to bridge the gap. Back on my own with the kids, I started to try and make some contact, particularly as my daughter was becoming a teenager and she wanted to spend more time with her mum. I did not want her to grow into an adult with bitterness. I wanted her and my sons to know that both parents loved them very much and that even though they lived with me, they had access and contact with the other parent whenever they wished. For this reason we moved to be nearer to Amanda, and we are now good friends and share the mutual interest and love of our children. It has taken ten years but at least they can start their adult life knowing there are two parents who are there for them.'

DISCUSSION POINTS

1. Sit down with your children and each of you compile a list of all the things you like doing on your own and with each other.

2. Look in national and local newspapers and magazines and see how lone parent families are portrayed.

3. Get your children discussing what they like and don't like doing at home.

Managing Your Personal Finances
How to achieve financial security
for yourself and your family
John Claxton

Life for most people has become increasingly beset by financial worries, and meanwhile the once-dependable prop of state help is shrinking. Today's financial world is a veritable jungle full of predators after your money. This book will help you to check your financial health and prepare a strategy towards creating your own welfare state and financial independence. Find out in simple language with many examples and case studies how to avoid debt, how to finance your home, how to prepare for possible incapacity or redundancy and how to finance your retirement, including care in old age. Discover how to acquire new financial skills, increase your income, reduce outgoings, and prepare to survive in a more self-reliant world. John Claxton is a chartered management accountant and chartered secretary; he teaches personal money management in adult education.

£8.99, 160 pp illus. paperback. 1 85703 328 0.

Available from How To Books Ltd, Plymbridge House,
Estover Road, Plymouth PL6 7PZ.
Customer Services Tel: (01752) 202301. Fax: (01752) 202331
Please add postage & packing (£1 UK, £2 Europe, £3 world airmail).

Credit card orders may be faxed or phoned.

6
Knowing Your Legal Rights

'Until I was on my own I had little contact with the law and I had never been to a solicitor. My ex-partner dealt with all things official. Suddenly I was fighting for the custody of my kids, the right to keep my home, and maintenance. After all this was resolved, my solicitor asked me whether I had written a will, and who was going to care for the children if anything happened to me. These things never occurred to me.'

Becoming a lone parent is a traumatic experience, and the emotional effects are difficult enough to contend with. However, you also need to be prepared for all the legal paperwork that can descend on you after relationship break-up. The law is there to protect and help you, although it may not always feel like that. You need to know and understand your legal rights, whether concerned with custody of your children, maintenance, keeping your home or getting one in the first place. Do not despair as legal advice and help with costs are readily available. However, gaining a good understanding of your legal rights will help you find the right help and ask the right questions, and will take away some of the unnecessary worry caused by the formal-looking legal letters which will haunt your letterbox.

UNDERSTANDING THE LEGAL IMPLICATIONS

You cannot avoid the law of the land. Even if you hid away in a remote Scottish island, you would still be covered by it. You can refer everything to a solicitor or go to a range of agencies that will provide legal advice, but the key is to open your eyes to your situation and first decide clearly what you want, then find out the legal implications and how you can achieve your goal. Your aim may be to get rid of a violent partner, to divorce your husband or wife, to obtain maintenance or secure your home. The law should be seen as a positive tool to help you. Yes, it can be confusing, long-winded and expensive, but it can work and protect your rights.

How much will it cost me?
Using the law does cost money, sometimes a great deal of money. Many people 'forget' about costs until legal battles are resolved, and then receive a shock. Legal costs can eat away all the gains you thought you had made.

Can I get any help with legal costs?
Legal Aid is available for those on low income but it is only really free if you end up with nothing, as the Legal Aid Board will recoup monies from any property or assets sold as a result of the relationship ending. It will effectively take a first charge.

Legislation

As a single parent you have the status and title of parent of a child or children, whether or not you were married. If you are in dispute with your ex-partner, whether it be over the custody of your children, ownership of your home, or getting a divorce, there are laws that will determine your rights. The law also affects the bereaved single parent. Below is a brief summary of the main legal provisions that may relate to your situation.

Note: Some of the forms used in legal proceedings are reproduced in the Appendix at the end of this book.

Married Women's Property Act 1882
Section 17 enables the court to decide on the property rights of husbands and wives.

Law of Property Act 1925
Section 30 enables a co-habiting man or woman to apply for the sale of the property which he or she co-owns with his or her partner.

Matrimonial Causes Act 1973
The main piece of legislation relating to divorce, setting out how a divorce can be obtained. It explains what financial orders can be made by the court and what considerations the court will take into account in deciding financial relief issues. (But note that all these provisions will be affected by the government's proposals to amend the divorce law—see below.)

Inheritance (Provision for the Family and Dependants) Act 1975
Enables a dependant to make a claim against the estate of a deceased

person who does not leave reasonable provision for the claimant in his or her will.

Domestic Violence and Matrimonial Proceedings Act 1976
One of the Acts enabling a cohabitee/spouse to apply for injunctions ordering the ex-partner to get out of the house or stop assaulting him or her.

Matrimonial Homes Act 1983
Provides a non-tenant spouse with rights of occupation and a non-tenant or joint-tenant spouse with the legal right to apply to the court for a transfer of the tenancy.

Child Abduction Act 1984
Establishes criminal sanctions in relation to children taken out of British jurisdiction.

Matrimonial and Family Proceedings Act 1984 (updated the Matrimonial Causes Act 1973)
Made clean breaks more likely. Enables people divorced outside England and Wales to apply for financial relief.

Children Act 1989
Provides the framework of law for all matters relating to children including residence, contact and finances.

Child Support Act 1991
Provides for a way to deal with maintenance payments for children. Established the Child Support Agency.

Pensions Act 1995
Creates the possibility of the court at the time of divorce earmarking a proportion of your ex-husband's private pension to be paid to you during his lifetime.

Review of divorce laws 1996
The government's proposals to reform the divorce laws are contained in the Family Law Bill, currently before Parliament. The main aim is to take the 'blame' or 'fault' out of divorce proceedings and encourage mediation between separating and divorcing couples, particularly in regard to children. Legal Aid will be available to pay for mediation if mediation is appropriate. There was a strong move to bring in a Family Homes and Domestic Violence Act which would

have given more rights to cohabitees who are not covered by the Matrimonial Homes Act, but this failed to get on the statute books. Hopefully this will be addressed in future years.

Note: There are other laws in Scotland and Northern Ireland which are relevant to single parents but they are not listed here.

DEALING WITH DIVORCE AND CUSTODY

Your marriage has ended and you are seeking divorce and custody of your children. The formality of divorce proceedings can be very traumatic as they transform your private life and former relationship into cold and meaningless legal phrases and bits of paper. The law uses words that may mean very little to you and often need translating into simple language.

Relationships end and couples live apart for some time before the legal process begins, and there is often uncertainty about who starts what. In the majority of cases the mother is awarded custody of her children and the husband is allowed 'reasonable access'. Arrangements for the children are outlined in the Statement of Arrangements for the children. See Appendix pp. 122–130.

What are court orders?
Court orders are a form of judgment that state what will happen to your child. There are four main orders:

- *Residence Order*—details who your child will live with.

- *Contact Order*—details the allowed contact of the other parent.

- *Specific Issue Order or Prohibited Steps Order*—allows one parent to prevent the custodial parent from doing things they object to, eg moving abroad, or changing their name.

- *Family Assistance Order*—not usually used, but allows the court to appoint a social worker or another family member to advise on the upbringing of the child. Could be used for teenage mums.

Child Support Agency
All questions involving regular payments for the maintenance of children, whether you have been married or not, are dealt with by the Child Support Agency, established under the Child Support Act

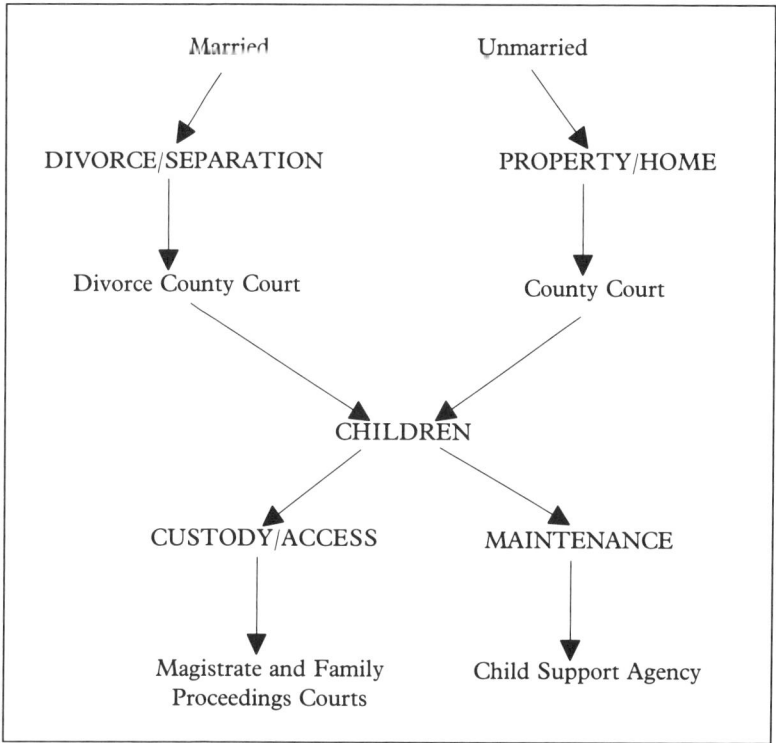

Fig. 2. The single parent route through the legal system.

1991. All parents must contribute financially to the upbringing of their children. If you receive benefit from the state, you will have to provide details of the father or mother of your children, and the CSA will pursue them for payment.

Courts
The courts now decide which court is best for children's cases, so it doesn't matter in which court such cases start. Fig. 2 is a simplified guide to the single parent route through the legal system.

Magistrates and Family Proceedings Courts
Family cases are held in private and the courts deal with:

1. Married adults' applications for separation and maintenance orders and for lump sum payments to a maximum of £1,000.

2. Any application for residence, contact, parental responsibility,

specific issues, prohibited steps, adoption or lump sum payment (max. £1,000) order in respect of or for a child.

3. Mothers' applications to decide the paternity of children.

4. Any application for protection against domestic violence by people who live together, whether married or not.

County and Divorce County Courts
All cases which involve divorce and separation.

The Family Division of the High Courts
All appeals and referrals from County Court and Family Proceedings Courts. All original applications to make a child a ward of court.

ACKNOWLEDGING THE LEGAL RIGHTS OF THE OTHER PARENT

Whether you have been married or not, the legal position of your children is of prime importance, and you need to know your legal rights to your children and the rights of the other parent. This is an area that can give rise to bitter disputes and legal battles over custody. Chapter 2 explains the concept of parental responsibility as outlined in the Children Act 1989, the main law which protects the interests of your child. The Act defines who has the right to be the legal parent of your child and which parent has the full responsibility.

All mothers and married fathers have automatic legal rights to their children and have legal responsibility for them. Unmarried fathers do not have an automatic right although under the Child Support Act, they have a duty to maintain the child.

When could issues relating to children give rise to legal disputes?
● You have been married and are now divorcing.

● You have been living with your child's other parent and the relationship has ended.

● You have never lived together with your child's other parent and cannot agree arrangements between yourselves, eg the unmarried father wants to see his child.

● Other people have concerns about the children and either wish to have access to them or wish to take them into their care. This could include grandparents, a former foster parent, or the local Social Services Department. If you are concerned about your children being put into care, you need urgently to seek detailed advice and you should contact your local Citizens' Advice Bureau or law centre.

Can the unmarried father of my child get legal rights of responsibility?
Yes. There are several ways. Either the mother makes a Parental Responsibility agreement with the father, or the father applies to the court for a Parental Responsibility Order. The latter can be complex as the father has to prove he is the other parent and put up a very strong case that the Order is in the best interest of the child. Such action is often necessary when the mother has left the child in the care of the unmarried father and the school or local Social Services have questioned his legal rights to the child.

Does the unmarried father of my child have any rights?
If you are not married to the child's father he does not have an automatic right to custody or access, and if you don't want him to have such rights, it will be necessary for him to obtain a court order. He still has to pay maintenance.

I have a maintenance order against the father of my child, but I feel it is not in our best interests for him to have access
A father must pay maintenance for his child, but if he wants to have access he has to apply separately to the courts for a contact order. Maintenance is dealt with separately by the Child Support Agency. You have the right to object to his application.

I am frightened that my ex-husband will abduct my children
If your husband has access to the children and you fear that they might be abducted by your ex-partner, you can have them made wards of court or apply for an injunction preventing their removal.

FIGHTING TO KEEP YOUR HOME

Having a decent roof over your head is a crucial issue for all single parents. It is often a continual worry. You may have been living with your partner when the relationship ended, then he/she left but wants the house sold to gain access to his/her share of the capital. The ex-partner stops paying the mortgage and you cannot continue paying it. You have a council house in joint name, but you have to leave your home because of violence and find yourself homeless. All these are familiar stories for single parents and a key priority is to get a secure home for you and your children.

The important thing for you to know is that the issue of the home is very closely linked to the issue of the children. All children are protected by the Children Act 1989, which ensures children a right to a secure home over their head. You need to clarify your housing status and make sure that your house, whether mortgaged or rented, is transferred into your name. This will usually be done through the divorce process if you are married, but if you are not you will have to seek advice and possibly take the matter to court. You should seek advice from your local Housing Advice Centre, normally linked to the local authority, or the Citizens' Advice Bureau.

You own or rent your home in your sole name
As long as you are not in mortgage or rent arrears, your home is secure.

You own or rent your home jointly with your ex-partner
If you are married you need to get the building society or landlord to agree for you to remain in the property and if you rent you need to get the tenancy transferred into your name. This would usually be done through the courts.

If you are unmarried your position can be more difficult. You need to get your partner to agree to a transfer, and if there is a disagreement you may have to go to court.

Your home is owned or rented in your partner's sole name
As a married person with the responsibility of the children, you have the right to live in the matrimonial home, and this would be resolved through the divorce process. If unmarried, you would need to get proper legal advice, and if you rent you need to persuade the landlord to transfer the tenancy.

You have become homeless
If you are made homeless, the local authority has a statutory duty to assist you and provide a home. It is better to have contacted them in advance if you know you might lose your home as they can register you on the council housing list and nominate you to housing associations. You may have to put up with being in bed and breakfast accommodation initially, but it varies from area to area. Contact your local housing authority or the Citizens' Advice Bureau.

FINDING THE RIGHT LEGAL ADVICE

To know your legal rights you need to know where to get advice and what questions to ask.

Where do I get legal advice?
- solicitor

- local law centre

- housing aid centre

The main source of legal advice and assistance is solicitors, but it is often best to start with organisations that specialise in general or specific advice. For instance, if you have housing problems, go to your local housing advice centre first as they could point you towards a solicitor who specialises in housing law. Often organisations have solicitors attached to them.

What can a solicitor do for me?
Solicitors advise you about the law, and help you decide the best course of action. They can act as an effective emotional screen between you and your ex-partner and hopefully reduce the areas of conflict between you.

Why do I need a solicitor?
- Getting your divorce.

- Sorting out problems over the children.

- Getting court orders for maintenance and division of property.

- Getting information about finances.

- Getting agreement about finances.

- Getting advice on the best way the problem can be solved. The solicitor may be able to point out things you had not thought of.

How do I find a suitable solicitor?
You need to find a solicitor who has relevant experience in the area of law you want advice on. For example, if you are seeking a divorce or need to get maintenance for your children, you need a solicitor

with experience of Family Law. Ask around a variety of sources and see if the same name comes up.

- Ask family and friends. Have they had good experiences with a local solicitor?

- Ask local one parent family support groups and other single parents.

- Consult the Solicitors Regional Directory at your local library or Citizens' Advice Bureau.

- Send a stamped addressed envelope to the Solicitors Family Law Association. See Useful Addresses.

- Consult a specialist organisation on a suitable local solicitor; for example, Housing Aid Centre for a housing issue.

How do I make sure I am getting a good solicitor?
Ask questions. All solicitors will usually give the first appointment free and you should use this to find out whether he/she is suitable for you. Often the personality, gender and age of the solicitor will be an important factor. You might feel more at home with an older man, or a woman.

CONTROLLING THE LEGAL PROCESS

It is your life that is being put through the legal wringer, and it is important for you to make sure that you keep control. Don't forget the reasons why you are going to court:

- to legally untangle your relationship

- to resolve who gets the children

- to get maintenance for the children

- to keep your home.

Remember to:

(a) know clearly what you want

(b) ask questions

(c) get second opinions and advice from support organisations

(d) ask about costs

(e) find the best and least conflicting route.

USING ALTERNATIVES TO A SOLICITOR

You don't have to use a solicitor and you can 'do it yourself'. It is possible that if you are in paid work, you are not entitled to Legal Aid and cannot afford the legal costs of what you need to do. It is still important, however, to get advice and your local Citizens' Advice Bureau and law centre can provide it free. You can also visit the court offices and they will tell you what procedures you have to follow. National and local single parent support groups can also assist and advise, and there are a range of specialist organisations that may help too, like the Children's Legal Centre. This way can be very time consuming but you can feel more in control, although remember that if you represent yourself in court you could be up against a very skilled lawyer.

If a way could be found not to go through the legal procedures and instead come to terms amicably, everyone would take this route. But life is not as simple as this. Conciliation services are good and these are outlined in Chapter 3, p. 34.

LOOKING AT THE LEGAL IMPLICATIONS OF DEATH

The main issue when a partner dies is the will and probate. Probate is the official validation of a will, and an application must be made to the nearest probate court for approval before the intentions of the deceased can be put into effect.

What if there is no will?
If you were married at the time of death you will usually inherit everything.

If you were not married to your partner, you should be able to claim money for you and your child as long as there is clear evidence of parentage and you were wholly or partly dependent on your ex-partner.

Do I need a solicitor?
Many people manage to go through this process without employing a solicitor and find the Probate Registry staff very helpful. However, if there are complications, it is important to consult a solicitor.

WRITING A WILL

Do you have a will? Have you changed it since your ex-partner left? It is hard to think the unthinkable, but something could happen to you, and without a will your children's welfare could be threatened. You need to identify clearly the person who will act as the guardian of your children in the event of your death. Perhaps you are happy for them to be cared for by the other parent, perhaps you are not. Or you may be a widow/widower yourself and not have any other relatives. You need to find someone who is willing to take this responsibility and carry out your wishes.

How will my children live financially?
This is a vital question. If you are on benefit, whoever takes care of them will be able to claim for them, but if you are in paid work it is a good idea to consider a life insurance policy, with the children as the named beneficiaries.

Do I have to pay a solicitor to write a will?
Usually, but you may be able to get Legal Aid. It is a good idea to consult a solicitor, but you can write a will yourself.

COPING WITH OTHER LEGAL BATTLES

The three principle issues that tend to affect single parents are the children, the home and money. Related to the last of these is a fourth area of legal concern if you get into debt and default on loans or credit agreements. This is covered in Chapter 7, the section on negotiating with creditors.

If you receive any legal letters that you don't understand, then go immediately to the CAB or contact single parent support groups and get someone to explain what is happening. You will get immediate relief as you will understand the situation more clearly and know what to do. Legal letters are always frightening and can be very threatening, but often they seem more frightening than they really are. Remember you have legal rights and are more protected than you may think. Don't let a legal letter get to you. Seek advice immediately.

DISCUSSION POINTS

1. Find out whether there is a local law centre. Enquire at the Citizens' Advice Bureau for a list of solicitors that specialise in family law.

2. Draw up a set of questions about your legal concerns and make initial appointments with two solicitors. Make sure the sessions are free. Compare their answers.

3. Work out the details of your will and think clearly how the children would be cared for in the event of your death.

7
Living on a Low Income

'Is my income adequate to cover our needs?'

This is the million dollar question that all single parents ask, as it's well known that single parenthood can seriously damage your wealth. The majority of lone parents, like you, face real hardships because of lack of money. Although many of you may escape the poverty trap, or hopefully, never have to experience it, all single parents discover very quickly that the system is stacked against them. Over one million of the 1.4 million single parents in the UK are on some form of state benefit.

Bringing up children is expensive, and there is still very little or no help towards childcare costs. As a single parent family, you have the disadvantage of there being only one adult, who not only has the social and domestic responsibility of bringing up your children but also potentially has to be the breadwinner as well. You may also have just survived a very traumatic divorce and separation that has left you seriously in debt.

UNDERSTANDING YOUR FINANCES

The important thing for you is to come to terms with your finances if you want to get in control of your life. You will be amazed what you can achieve when you start to understand your money. Here is a checklist to get you started on the road to better control.

- Write down your income against your expenditure. See the sample sheets on p. 74. Be absolutely honest!

- Do you owe money? Write a list of all you owe and to whom.

- Try to establish how you got into debt in the first place.

- Identify the essential debts/payments.

- If there are companies that you owe money to, keep them informed of any problems in meeting repayments.

- Go and talk to a money adviser, (see page 86), taking all the relevant information. Talking about your financial situation starts to enable you to understand it. It is not a social stigma any more to have financial problems.

WRITING AN INCOME AND EXPENDITURE CHECKLIST

Keeping a list of your expenditure and income sounds tedious but unless you have some idea of how much you are spending and on what, it is difficult to decide where you can cut down, and what you can really afford to pay on debts. Use the checklist on p. 74 to get you started. Are you spending enough on the right things?

CLAIMING ALL YOUR BENEFIT ENTITLEMENTS

It is essential that you claim every state benefit that you are entitled to. You may be on income support, and think you are receiving everything you should be getting. But don't take this for granted. Seek advice either from the Benefits Agency or from your local Citizens' Advice Bureau. If you are in paid work, you may not realise that you are still entitled to assistance. For example, you may have a low income and be eligible for Family Credit, housing and council tax benefit. Your children may be entitled to free school meals.

There are three main types of benefits available:

- income related
- housing related
- child centred.

Income related

Income Support
This is a means-tested benefit for people over 18 who are working no more than 16 hours per week and whose income is below a certain level. It can be used to top up part-time earnings, if you work less than 16 hours. As a single parent you are automatically entitled to claim this benefit.

You must have no more than £8,000 in savings. Savings of between £3,000 and £8,000 will affect the amount you receive.

You can also get help with financial emergencies, maternity

INCOME AND EXPENDITURE CHECKLIST

	Monthly/weekly	
Income	**At the moment**	**In the future**

Earnings
Child Benefit
One Parent Benefit
Maintenance
Income Support
Family Credit
Housing Benefit
Council Tax Benefit
Any other Income/benefit

TOTAL INCOME

Expenses
Rent/mortgage
Food
Council tax
Electricity
Gas
Other fuel costs
Childcare costs
Travel
Clothes
School meals
Work expenses
Newspapers/cigarettes
Social life
Debts (see checklist on p. 81)
Any other expenses

TOTAL EXPENSES

payments, help with funeral costs, cold weather payments, loans for essentials and crises, and free or reduced milk for the under-fives. Contact your local Benefits Agency.

Family Credit

If you work over 16 hours and are responsible for one or more children under 16, or under 19 if in full-time education, and have savings of less than £8,000, you could be entitled to Family Credit. If you have a weekly income of between £90 and £120 you could receive £40–£50 Family Credit. (See the Family Credit in Fig. 3). Contact your local Benefits Agency for further details.

Case study: Sue claims her entitlements

She works part time as a dinner nanny at a local school. She works 20 hours a week and earns £4.50 per hour. She is entitled to Family Credit and gains a further £80 per week. She receives Housing Benefit of 65 per cent of her rent. Sue receives maintenance from her ex-husband, but has recently contacted the Child Support Agency who are taking up her case. Sue has had problems with her teeth and as she is on Family Credit, her dental costs are paid by the state.

Childcare initiative

If you receive Family Credit you are entitled to receive further help towards childcare costs, if you pay for these through a childminder, nursery or Kid's club. Contact you local Benefits Agency for further details.

Housing related

Income Support

If you have a mortgage and are entitled to Income Support, only your mortgage interest will be covered. You have to wait two months before any mortgage interest is paid. For any mortgages taken out after October 1995, you will have to wait nine months.

Housing Benefit

Like Income Support this is also means tested. It is essentially to help pay the rent. You must have less than £16,000 in savings, and the amount of help you receive is dependent on income, size of family and savings. Contact your local housing authority and Benefits Agency. Claimants on Income Support receive maximum Housing and Council Tax Benefit.

Name.. Address...

Step 1: How much capital? (if over £8,000 no F.C. payable)		

Step 2: Work out maximum Family Credit		**Step 3:** Work out weekly income	

Step 2: Work out maximum Family Credit

Single parent/Couple	44.30
Children: Under 11	11.20
11 - 15	
16 - 17	
18 or over	
Sub-Total A	55.50

Step 3: Work out weekly income

Earnings

Claimant's (net)	120.00
Partner's (net)	
Sub-Total B	120.00

Benefits

Industrial Injuries	
Invalidity/SDA	
Retirement Pension	
SSP/SMP over 13 weeks	
Unemployment/sickness	
War Pension (£10 disregard)	
OTHER	
Sub-Total C	-

Other Income

Maintenance (· disregard)	
Tariff Income	
Occupational Pension	
Childminding Fees (disregard 2/3)	
OTHER	
Sub-Total D	-
TOTAL INCOME (B+C+D)	120.00

Fig. 3. Family credit calculator sheet.

Step 4: Family Credit Calculation

Total Weekly Income
(B+C+D)

| 120.00 |

minus

Threshold Figure

| 71.70 |

=

Difference Figure

| 48.30 |

Note: If income is equal to or less than the threshold figure maximum Family Credit (A) is payable.

Maximum Family Credit
(A)

| 55.50 |

minus

70% of Difference Figure

| 33.81 |

=

Family Credit

| 21.69 |

Note: sample figures are only a guide, and likely to change. Visit your local Benefits Agency for correct calculation.

Council Tax Benefit
Again this depends on individual circumstances, but many areas have a 25 per cent reduction on houses with only one adult.

Child centred

Child Benefit
This is payable for each child under 16 years, or until 19 if still in full-time education.

One Parent Benefit
You can claim this as soon as you start to bring up a child on your own. You cannot claim if you are living with someone as man and wife. You need to be separated for 91 consecutive days before you can claim.

Widowed Mother's Allowance
This is a taxable weekly benefit for widows. It is not age dependent but you have to be claiming Child Benefit for at least one child. Widowers with children are not eligible although there is a campaign to change this anomaly. You are also entitled to Widow's Payment (a lump sum of 1,000).

All the above are outlined in detail in leaflets published by the Department of Social Security and available from your local DSS or Benefits Agency Office. There could be other entitlements that are not outlined above and relate to your particular circumstances.

CLAIMING MAINTENANCE FROM THE OTHER PARENT

Maintenance normally involves regular payments from a parent who is no longer living with the children to help towards paying for their everyday needs.

Maintenance arrangements were once dealt with solely by the courts. Since April 1993, under the Child Support Act, there is a new system for arranging child maintenance. The Child Support Agency (CSA), which comes under the Department of Social Security, assesses, collects and enforces the payment of child maintenance. You must still use the courts if you need to claim maintenance for yourself as the CSA only deals with maintenance for children.

Will receiving maintenance affect my benefits?
It depends on the benefit and the amount of maintenance. If you are

claiming Income Support your benefit will be reduced by £1 for every £1 you got in maintenance.

How is the maintenance calculated?
There is a formula for calculating maintenance which takes into account the individual circumstances of the family and the absent parent. These include:

- The day-to-day living expenses of the person with care and the children for whom the assessment is being made, plus housing costs.

- The day-to-day living expenses of the absent parent and any 'natural' children (ie children by birth or adoption but not stepchildren) living with them, plus housing costs.

- The net incomes of the absent parent and yourself.

Both parents are responsible for supporting their children.

How is the money paid?
It can be paid to you directly, via the CSA or the courts.

Note: See Chapter 6 on how to seek legal advice about claiming maintenance.

GETTING OUT OF DEBT

You owe money to friends and relatives, you've defaulted on your credit cards and the mortgage is in arrears. Every day you're expecting the bailiffs to arrive on your doorstep demanding immediate payment or your furniture—if you still have any! You're not alone—but you need help.

- Divorce is one of the main reasons people get into debt.

- Over 2 million people in the UK have debt problems.

- Multiple debt is very common—the average is 4 debts per household.

These days it's all too easy to be tempted to borrow more than you can afford. Between 1980 and 1990 the number of credit cards in circulation nearly tripled from 11.6 million to 29.8 million. You can be tempted to over-borrow if:

- you suddenly overspend

- the car or washing machine breaks down

- your house is burgled

- your earnings are lost through ill health or redundancy

- you separate or divorce.

No one sets out deliberately to get into debt but any one of these will put you at risk.

Act now! By admitting you have a problem you are well on the way to finding a solution.

Case study: Sally gets help with debt problems

Sally had debt problems, and owed over £3,000 to a credit company and her bank. She went to her local Citizens' Advice Bureau and drew up an Income and Expenditure list. She signed an agreement with the CAB, to allow them to write to her creditors on her behalf. She was able to offer £1 per month for one debt of £1,000. This was accepted.

Working out your debts

Sort out your debts into priority and non-priority (see the checklist in Fig. 4). Priority debts include:

- rent or mortgage

- service charges—gas, electricity, water, telephone

- council tax

- fines and court orders.

These are the ones to deal with first as you must keep a roof over your head.

Non-priority debts include:

- hire purchase

Details of priority expenditure arrears

These are debts owed to priority services that you require
to continue and that have power to cease these services or take
legal action easily to get you to repay.

	Arrears/ balances	*Normal repayments*	*Agreed repayments*
Rent council/private			
Mortgage 1st			
Other mortgages			
Loans			
Hire purchase			
Gas			
Electricity			
Telephone			
Council tax			
Others			

TOTALS

Non-priority credit debts/arrears

These should include credit cards, non-secured consumer
credit loans or bank overdrafts, store cards, clothing clubs, etc.

Name of company   *Money owed*

TOTALS

Fig. 4. Debt checklist.

Dear Creditors,

CREDIT AGREEMENT No. 1243

I am writing to let you know that I am having financial difficulties because I am a single parent and have fallen on hard times that mean I cannot keep up with the repayments.

My income is £100 per month. I have enclosed a financial statement so you can see how things stand. I can afford to pay you £7 each month. I should be grateful if you would consider freezing the interest on my loan for a short while so that I can pay back the original amount. If my financial situation changes, I will let you know.

If you agree to this arrangement, please let me know how you would like payments to be made.

I would like to make all future payments on the 5th of each month.

I am sorry for any inconvenience this may cause and hope that you will agree to my request.

Yours faithfully,

Fig. 5. Sample letter to creditor.

- store/credit cards

- bank/building society loans and overdrafts

- catalogue repayments.

Cut up your credit cards or send them back.

From your income and expenditure chart (p. 74), work out how much you can afford each creditor, aiming to pay each one something. A regular payment of £2 a month is better than nothing at all. Allocate the money on a pro rata basis.

The more you owe the creditor, the larger the payment must be. You need to inform all your creditors of your financial position.

Name . . . .

Address . . . .

. . . .

Income
Wages (after deduction) . . . .   £ . . . . .
Benefits . . . .   £ . . . . .
Other . . . .   £ . . . . .
Total . . . .   £ . . . . .

Essential spending
Rent/mortgage . . . .   £ . . . . .
Gas . . . .   £ . . . . .
Electricity . . . .   £ . . . . .
Other fuel . . . .   £ . . . . .
Water charges . . . .   £ . . . . .
Household insurance . . . .   £ . . . . .
Council tax/rates . . . .   £ . . . . .
Food . . . .   £ . . . . .
Clothing . . . .   £ . . . . .
Travel to work . . . .   £ . . . . .
Childcare . . . .   £ . . . . .
Other spending . . . .   £ . . . . .
Total . . . .   £ . . . . .
Emergencies . . . .   £ . . . . .

Total . . . .   £ . . . . .

What's left over . . . .   £ . . . . .

List of creditors and how much I owe

. . . .   £ . . . . .
. . . .   £ . . . . .

I can pay your company . . . .   £ . . . . .

Fig. 6. Sample financial statement.

NEGOTIATING WITH CREDITORS

You are not going to get rid of your debt problem by running away from your creditors! It is dangerous to ignore them. The problem won't go away, and you will risk being taken to court, with all the stress and worry that entails. The only way you are going to avoid this kind of stress is to negotiate with your creditors—talk to them either directly or preferably through a debt counsellor.

How will they respond?
When you fall into arrears with payments through no fault of your own, the problem will be handled both sympathetically and positively by all reputable finance houses and companies. Beware of loan sharks! It is important to get advice (see the next section).

How do I negotiate?
You must find out whom to write to, preferably by name, and point out the following:

- You fully intend to repay your outstanding debt.

- You have worked out a plan to repay your debt.

- All your creditors will be repaid an amount proportionate to your outstanding debt.

- You can afford to pay x amount monthly.

(See the sample letter in Fig. 5 and the sample financial statement in Fig. 6.)

What happens if I am taken to court?
You will have to provide details of your income and expenditure and the court will fix an amount probably similar to the one you suggest. It can work in your favour as the court will freeze the amount owed and no further interest will be payable on it.

What happens if a debt collector comes to my door?
A credit company has to inform you in writing that they may visit and this has to be during reasonable hours, and they cannot embarrass you on the doorstep or in front of your children. Do not be harassed. Tell them that you cannot give them an answer at that time and you need to seek advice. If they are persistent, call the police. Many

reputable companies like British Telecom use debt collection agencies and some sell on your debts. They have to work within the law. Get advice immediately if you are in this position as it can cause unnecessary distress.

INCREASING YOUR INCOME

There are lots of ways of increasing income and it is worth exploring whether any are appropriate to you and your situation.

Do you have a spare room in the house you could rent out? This could give you an income and perhaps company.

Many single parents do a number of part-time jobs as opposed to working full time. Do you have hidden talents, such as writing, which could be done at home?

Case study: Martin finds part-time work
Martin gave up his full-time job to look after his children, and had to claim Income Support. He can earn up to £15 a week before this affects his benefit. Martin works three hours a week in a local youth club, and is paid £5 an hour. He is able to take his children along, and thus earns some extra money as well as actively involving the children.

SINGLE PARENTS AND TAX

Lone parents who are working will have to pay tax, calculated on the income received in the 'tax year' which runs from 6 April of one year to 5 April of the next year. Each year people are allowed certain amounts of income which are not taxed. These are called tax allowances.

Lone parents are entitled to two tax allowances:

1. The single person's allowance is £3,525 in 1995/96 and means that the first £3,525 you earn is not taxed.

2. The additional personal allowance means that on the next £1,720 of your earnings your tax is reduced to 15p in the £1. This gives you equality with married couples who have a similar allowance.

Widows have an additional bereavement allowance for up to two years after the death of their husband and then have the single person's and additional personal allowance.

If you are working, it is important that you inform the tax office that you are a single parent to make sure you receive the additional personal allowance.

GETTING ADVICE AND SUPPORT

Do get advice on your debt problems. A third party, such as the Citizens' Advice Bureau, will get a better response from your creditors and help to ease your mind. It will mean that your creditors will have to recognise that they are not the only organisation that you owe money to and that you have limited means. Do not be embarrassed —the majority of people in the UK have debts and thousands have serious debt problems.

You can get free help from your local Citizens' Advice Bureau or Trading Standards Department. Some have Money Advice Centres specially to deal with financial problems. Look in the phone book for the addresses. Trading Standards Departments are part of local authorities. They are sometimes known as Consumer Protection Departments. Look under your authority's name, or, in Northern Ireland, the Department of Economic Development.

There is also a National Debtline Service, 318 Summer Lane, Birmingham B19 3RL. Tel. (0121) 359 8501. A useful organisation called Creditcure Voluntary Association, 109 Bramford Rd, Ipswich IP1 2LP produces a newsletter and a debt-surviving manual (send SAE).

CONTROLLING YOUR MONEY

Although not easy, you will get great satisfaction from gaining greater control over your money. Lone parenthood often gives rise to a lot of guilt, and many of us spend lavishly on our children when in fact we haven't got enough money to do so. Remember, your children need *you* not the gifts you can buy. Great enjoyment can be had from making toys, cooking special economy meals together, going for a walk in the park. Many cinemas have children's clubs showing films at low cost. Don't hide things from the children. Make them part of the exercise and you will be surprised what savings ideas they have. They may want to hire a video—try the video hire at your local library, half the price of the high street shops. The best way to control your money is not to rush into things. Take time, think about your budget, talk to people/advice agencies.

- Budget to save each month, however little.

- Harden up. Decide what you really need to have a reasonable lifestyle.

- When you go out, take just enough cash to cover your planned purchases.

- Make a note of everything you buy, and the price. Encourage your children to do the same.

- Avoid 'buy now, pay later' purchases.

- If you have credit cards, put them away for real emergencies, or get rid of them.

- If you have to borrow, always check the APR (annual percentage rate). The lower the rate, the less interest you pay. Look out for interest-free arrangements.

DISCUSSION POINTS

1. Check whether you are receiving all the income you are entitled to. Make an appointment with the Benefit Agency or Citizens' Advice Bureau.

2. Draw up an income and expenditure and a debt checklist.

3. Find out where you could get debt counselling/advice locally. Contact your Citizens' Advice Bureau.

8
Coping with the Stress of Being a Single Parent

'Each year six million people consult their doctor because they feel depressed or anxious. It is quite normal, and lone parents do not live in a stress-free zone.'

Being a parent is stressful in itself, but taking the full burden of parental responsibility means taking on the stress levels of two people. You do not have a partner to help share the care of your children or any of the very basic household duties.

When the children are ill, and you have to go to your part-time job, there is no one to cover. When you are tired in the morning and want to roll over, you still have to get up and make the breakfast. The simplest unexpected event can throw your whole world into turmoil, and you have no other adult to calm you down.

There is no easy solution. Even finding a new partner and creating a new step-family situation does not ease things. The high failure rate in second relationships shows that starting afresh can be just as stressful. However, this book is not about doom and gloom, it is about finding positive ways that will help you come to terms with your situation, turn negative situations into positive ones. The aim is to provide ideas and suggestions on how to make your life more rewarding and happy, and that means getting your stress levels down.

Surveys show that financial difficulties, work, illness, unemployment, children, and personal relationships are the six factors most responsible for stress. Single parents often have all six, and do not have the benefit of a partner with whom to share their worries.

LEARNING TO SEE THE POSITIVE VIEW

Some people thrive on stress, and deal with it very successfully. But what happens when your life becomes more and more stressful so that you feel unable to cope? You need to take action, because stress builds up and can result in physical illness. Too much stress in your life often leads to headaches, insomnia, depression, irritability, tiredness and lower resistance to infections—colds, flu and cold sores are prime examples. The problem with stress is that many people try to combat it by turning to alcohol, coffee and tea, cigarettes, bingeing or not eating, and drugs both prescribed and illegal. While some of these may offer temporary relief, they actually make the situation worse.

TALKING TO YOUR CHILDREN

We all need to talk and we need friends. Do not overlook the fact that your closest friends are there with you in your home—your children. They see your stress, and even if they are very young, they are concerned for you since they love you. You are their homemaker and protector. Your well-being is extremely important to them, and a stressed-out and deeply depressed parent is going to worry them, make them react in a variety of ways that could cause more stress for you. See them as a positive source of support. It is not a question of them against you, although it seems that way at times. Talk to them, tell them the truth about why you are stressed, get them on your side and positively working with you not against you.

PLANNING YOUR LIFE

What you have to do is get down to the root causes, if you can, and also find ways of relieving the symptoms and helping yourself to cope.

To begin with, examine the areas in your life that are most stressful and try to work out some solutions and alternatives. The simple event of not being able to find your keys as you are leaving the house causes your stress levels to rise, as you are made late by searching for them. What easy step could you take to ensure this is not a daily problem? All situations can be resolved. It is in your power.

Don't be overwhelmed by what you have to do. Make lists and break jobs down into stages. It's quite a good idea to have daily, weekly and monthly plans for what you want to achieve. Don't set yourself impossible goals and be prepared to be flexible. Ticking items off on your plans as you go along brings a sense of achievement and helps you feel much more in control.

TALKING WITH OTHERS

Stress is often caused because you bottle it up, hiding it from yourselves and others. You become afraid to talk about your problems.

Always remember that what you are feeling is being felt by

thousands of others, and a problem shared is a problem spared. The simple act of talking honestly and openly about your situation can be a great relief. It often has the effect of putting everything into perspective, especially when friends describe how they are feeling the same and tell you how they are trying to overcome similar problems.

Who do I talk to?
Relatives, friends, your local doctor (who can refer you for counselling), advice lines and lone parent support groups.

GETTING THE CHILDREN TO WORK WITH YOU

You have a child or children who are part of your team. They may fight, argue, stamp their feet, and at times make your life a misery. But they are yours and your team. Get them to work with you. Simple chores around the home can be made fun and children like doing things. They might not do things the way you want them and not as efficiently, but they have to learn. Think of what your mum or dad did with you, and how you helped them.

GETTING SUPPORT IN A CRISIS

Realising you need support in a crisis often only dawns on you when you're in the middle of one. It may be your child being ill at school and you cannot get to the school to pick him or her up. It can be finding out that your child has a day off school and you have to work. You may be ill and bedridden, and have no one to look after the children. You may just be at the end of your tether and need to talk to someone.

There are a range of local support contacts such as your doctor and social services as well as national support organisations that can advise on solutions. Start now to build a network of support so that when something *does* go wrong you can call on someone.

DEVELOPING SUPPORT NETWORKS

Gingerbread, Span (Single Parent Action Network) and the National Council for One Parent Families can provide information on local one parent family support groups. Many such groups offer help and counselling for parents via a telephone help line and a range of written advice. They are sometimes staffed by professionals from a variety of backgrounds who can help find reasonable solutions for family problems. There are also often a range of informal networks around schools, playgroups, community centres and churches. Explore what is best for you, talk to people and ask questions.

Develop your own group by asking friends around to your home and discuss each other's problems and how you can help each other.

DISCUSSION POINTS

1. Write a list of things you like doing and plan a week where you include at least one hour of activity a day which you do on your own.

2. Draw up a list of all the contact numbers you need in a crisis, including friends, the school, doctor, parents, dentist, local parent support group, Gingerbread. Put the list up somewhere so that you can see it in an emergency.

3. Find out all the local support groups that are relevant to you. Ask your local Citizens' Advice Bureau and library.

9
Working and Caring for Children

'For many there is no option but to find work as well as caring for their children. I could have stayed on Income Support. I was poor but able to manage. Many of my lone parent friends could not. The reality was that I was going mad just looking after my sons, I needed to do something away from them. My job gives me a sense of fulfilment and independence. It is a lot of hassle getting the children to school and then myself to work. Holidays and illness can be a nightmare. But I felt completely lost when I was just at home. Some parents can't bear to leave their children, I am not one of these people. For me this is the best option, and I am a better mother for doing it.'

As a full-time parent, you have a full-time job bringing up your children. This is an important role. Be proud of it. However, you need money to live. As a single parent, your three most likely sources of income, unless you have private savings or investments, are earned income, maintenance payments and state benefits.

The main reasons for you to work are to earn enough to live, to provide for your children and to improve your standard of living. Working can also be enjoyable and enable you to develop. It breaks the isolation, enables you to meet others. The key is to balance all these needs with the need to care for your children. The physical and emotional demands of parenting can clash with work and coping singlehanded makes this more likely. However, it is not necessarily easier with a partner, as even in two parent families most parenting usually falls to one parent. Many working single parents actually feel less hasseled and more in control than they did when they lived with a partner and had to come home and look after them too!

It is not easy bringing up children alone as well as taking the extra strain of working, but it is the way to more independence, and it is likely that the government will develop policies that encourage more single parents to follow this route. There are already benefits that enable you to top up your salary and assistance towards childcare costs.

DO YOU NEED TO WORK?

Paid work often provides a sense of status. The lack of work status can be a traumatic experience, but you must feel positive about yourself and realise that you are doing a very important job by bringing up your child or children. However, you may need to work for financial reasons or because you want an identity outside the home.

There may be many reasons why you are thinking of going into paid work, quite apart from the need to earn money and the wish to become financially independent. These could include:

● getting to meet people

● using your past experience

● increasing your self-confidence

● following a career

● status

● self respect/self fulfilment

● planning your financial future

● something to offer.

Will I be better off if I work?
Because wages for available work are often very low, lone parents can find there is a fine line between whether they will be better or worse off by doing paid work. You will need to take into account all the possible sources of income from wages, benefits, maintenance, grants and allowances and compare these against all your expenses. Be realistic about your expenses, and don't forget the extra expenses of employment, such as clothing, travel and childcare.

FINDING FULFILMENT OUTSIDE THE HOME

There are some who are extremely happy 'just' being a homemaker and parent, but many feel the pressure on one person causes isolation and frustration. You are like a battery and you need recharging with stimulation and ideas in order to feel positive and motivated. It can be a simple process of meeting other adults and contributing to an activity which is not focused on your own children.

Case study: Martin gets involved in youth work

Martin Lewis does youth work in a local club one night a week. He gets paid £15 a week which is the allowable level of pay without affecting his Income Support. 'The job is only three hours a week, but it is important to me as it has given me an identity away from my home. It enables me to say to people that I am a youth worker and lone parent. I take my children with me. The club is lively and the other workers have become good friends. I am now training in youth work and hope to gain a qualification. It has opened a door for me and developed skills I didn't know I had.'

EXPLORING THE OPTIONS

You need to have an open mind and explore all possibilities. You have the opportunity to think of what you want to do, and you should avoid limiting yourself. There are a range of options which could put you on to the road to work, whether looking for an existing job, retraining and updating skills, going to college, working or establishing a business from home, or taking a part-time job that could lead on to full-time work.

There is a change in attitudes amongst employers in regard to making employment practices more flexible to enable parents and women in general to be able to return to work. These include job sharing, flexible hours, and workplace crèches. Investigate all the opportunities and see what route would best fit your needs. If you are already in a job, and are finding it detrimental to your home life, think about how you could improve things.

Case study: Martin re-examines his priorities

Martin was in a well-paid job, but as a senior manager his hours made it impossible to balance this with caring for the children. 'I tried so hard. I used every form of childcare from au pairs to kids' clubs, but I still got exhausted. I admire women who can balance the domestic side with working. I could not. I decided to go for counselling and was advised to re-examine my life and what my priorities were. I initially ignored this as I felt I had to maintain my job at all costs as I did not know what I would do if I lost it. I did lose my job in the end because my work deteriorated and my bosses had no sympathy with the situation I was in. To be fair I let the situation get out of hand. I had to pick myself up and re-examine my skills. I decided that my priorities are my children and I should find work that fits my circumstances and will build up possibilities when the children are older. I also needed to find a new home as I lost ours due to mortgage arrears. I now work one evening a week in a youth club, caretake a small church which provides us with a lovely tied cottage, and am starting to study on a part-time basis. I hope to make the step from Income Support to Family Credit by increasing my youth work hours. I am happier overall than I was when I tried to hold down my full-time job and as I don't have the childcare expenses, our living standard surprisingly has improved.'

How do I go about finding a job?
There are many sources of information on local employment and training opportunities. If you want to find out more, visit agencies and organisations mentioned. Libraries usually keep local and national newspapers and specialised journals. By finding out more about local opportunities you will expand your knowledge of what is available for you to choose from. You may also find jobs you have never thought of which will offer a chance to use your abilities.

Where to look
- employment agencies

- Jobcentres

- libraries and career advice centres

- unemployed workers centres

- vacancy boards, shop windows

- community notice boards (in libraries, stores, etc.)

- word of mouth, ask friends, people you know.

What to read
- local papers

- free papers

- national daily papers

- Sunday papers

- journals

- specialised papers/journals

- local authority vacancy lists

- local 'what's on' magazines.

What about volunteering?
This is a good initial option, as it enables you to get into work patterns and meet people. All charities rely on volunteers and it is acceptable to do voluntary work whilst receiving Income Support. Many organisations have training courses for volunteers that could lead on to full-time work. Often voluntary work enables you to discover skills you didn't know you had, and can lead you to raise your expectations about what you would like to do. Many lone parents do voluntary work, whether running a playgroup, assisting in a school or running a charity shop. Without them many organisations would fold.

What have I got to offer?
You have a lot to offer but need to sit down and evaluate your skills. Use the worksheet on p. 97 to discover your real potential.

GOING INTO FURTHER EDUCATION

Your first step to getting a job may be going to college or on a training scheme. Most areas have an adult advisory service offering guidance and information on careers and training at local and national level. Jobcentres have information on government training schemes and return to work initiatives such as job clubs. Colleges and adult education centres (which run a wide range of part-time and full-time courses), community centres, unemployed workers centres and various local centres also run classes and training courses.

Local libraries also have reference books, leaflets and addresses. There may be a special information service attached to the main library. Advice centres, Jobcentres, Social Services and education departments have information on grants, training allowances and other financial help.

Case study: Sally Hunt starts college
'Before Adam was born, I was a secretary and I hated it. I dreaded

---

Identifying experience and skills worksheet

Activity   *Experience, skills and knowledge*

Paid/unpaid employment

Voluntary activities

Leisure activities/interests

Positions of responsibility

---

every morning I had to go to work, I was so bored. More to the point, the money was terrible. I knew I could never afford to feed and clothe a baby on the wages. The major drawback was that I wasn't qualified or trained to do anything else. So I decided that I would study for a better job, one that I would be happy in and would enable me to provide a better future for my, as yet, unborn child. By chance I saw an advertisement in our local newspaper for a college quite near to home to study graphic design. I had always been good at art and I am always drawing. I'm ever so happy, as I really enjoy the course. It is really good to do things away from Adam, at the same time knowing he is alright. I feel I have a future for me and Adam.'

How do I find out about courses?
Your local library will have information about courses and where your local careers advice centre is located. Your local Training and Enterprise Council (TEC) will also be able to help and may have information on Access courses particularly targeted at lone parents and women. Most areas now have Women Returner courses that are a good insight into what work is available and provide assessment of your potential skills.

Will I get any financial help as a student?
If you initially go to college part time, you could remain on Income Support, but if you go full time you would be entitled to apply to your local education authority for a student award, which will include a Single Parent award, plus dependants and maintenance allowance. These would be paid in three instalments over the year. You can also apply for a student loan.

Will I get any help with childcare?
Many colleges now have crèches that are either free to students or at a low cost. Ask about this when applying for courses.

MOVING FROM BENEFIT TO WORK

If you are on Income Support and intend to work 16 hours or more a week you need to plan carefully. Look carefully at what your situation is at the moment and work out how much you need to earn to be better off going out to work. This is the big question for many single parents on Income Support (nearly two-thirds of all single parents in the UK). Government reports have noted that 90 per cent of these parents want to work but are often prevented by being financially worse off in work than if remaining on Income Support and by the lack of childcare.

How do I check whether it is viable for me to work or remain on benefit?
The Benefits Agency, Jobcentres and Citizens' Advice Bureau can help you in calculating whether you will be better off if you take a job.

Will I still be able to get some form of benefit?
If your earnings are below a certain limit, you will be entitled to Family Credit, Housing Benefit and Council Tax Benefit. (See Chapter 7, page 73.)

WORKING FROM HOME

Many jobs can be completely impractical, and costly. You need to find work that provides useful income but also is flexible enough to enable you to combine work with being a parent. Working from home can be an effective way of combining roles and there are a variety of ways of doing this. You can start a business or work for another business that uses homeworkers. Being a childminder is a form of

Ideas for working from home

Childminding   knitting   clothes-selling parties

hat-making   selling children's books and toys

making theatrical costumes   bookbinding   crochet

dress-making   candle-making

decorating glass   flower-making   patchwork

embroidery   jewellery   picture-framing

soft toys   baking and cake making   secretarial services

printing   bookkeeping

writing   painting   party catering

compiling crosswords   making sandwiches

beauty consultant   dried flowers   bed and breakfast

hairdressing   photography

graphic design   proofreading   driving instructor

language tuition   typing

au pair agency   contact and pen pal club

self-employment and many lone parents find this a viable way of caring for their children and earning money by looking after others. If you have secretarial skills, you could offer your services to local small businesses.

The ideas in the box above are real things that many lone parents do from home, and there are lots of other ideas. If you wish to explore this option you need to get advice. Find out about your local business advice centre through your local Jobcentre, Citizens' Advice Bureau or the local library. Your local Training and Enterprise Council

(TEC) will provide a range of courses and information for people seeking work and wishing to explore a business idea. It is important to try your idea out amongst friends. If you are on benefit, it won't affect benefit whilst you are experimenting with ideas, as long as you are not making large amounts of money and not declaring it. Many childminders still receive Income Support quite legitimately.

BALANCING YOUR HOME LIFE WITH WORK

You need to have strong discipline to combine home and work life, as both can be very demanding. Any working single parent will tell you about the sheer exhaustion of getting up, feeding the kids, getting them to school or childminder, arriving at work on time—and then the reverse trip at the end of the day. Many single parents work in the evenings and at weekends, and this means they have very little time on their own. You need to think very carefully about developing a way that enables you to rest properly, as the pressures could and will cause extreme stress.

Survival checklist for working lone parents

● Accept offers of help.

● Build up a strong support network of people you can rely on.

● If you're going through the process of separation or divorce, or have been bereaved, take things slowly, one step at a time.

● Get advice about benefits, pensions or maintenance entitlements and make sure you claim.

● Look for training or retraining opportunities to maximise your earning capacity.

● Cut down on guilt feelings and focus on the positive aspects of your situation.

● Go for childcare that offers the maximum stress relief within your budget.

● Look for a family-friendly employer or convert your existing workplace into one.

DISCUSSION POINTS

1. Find out all you can about local employment opportunities and sources of information on training, courses and jobs.

2. Complete an experience and skills worksheet.

3. Think about what you would do if you worked from home. Do you have any skills that could earn you money?

10
Finding Local Childcare

A primary need for all single parents is good, local and inexpensive childcare. The reality is that in most areas childcare provision is limited and expensive with inflexible hours. However, there is a slow growth and the government (local and national) and the private sector are recognising the need for good childcare if skilled parents are to be encouraged to return to work and to stay.

The options for childcare, whether you are in employment or training, intend to go back to college, or just need time on your own, are your support network (family and friends), voluntary sector provision such as playgroups and after-school clubs, paid child-minders, or private or state nurseries.

Finding good childcare is vital because it enables you to meet other needs, including continuing in work, getting a job, seeking further education or giving time to yourself. For some lone parents, *providing* childcare, as childminders, is a source of income—a case of 'well I've got to look after mine, why don't I earn money looking after other children in my own home.'

USING FRIENDS AND FAMILY

It can be the ideal solution if a close friend or relative lives locally and is willing to help. But remember that informal arrangements like these can have their own problems—a relative may feel they cannot say no and over a period of time may feel put upon especially if there is no payment involved.

FINDING OUT ABOUT LOCAL CHILDCARE PROVISION

Following the Children Act 1989, Social Services have a duty to register daycare facilities for children under 8 including childminders, whilst taking children up to the age of 14 into consideration. The legal provisions include crèches and out-of-school care. All facilities should be reviewed every three years. Social Services should therefore be a good source of local up-to-date information. Most of them respond very swiftly to initial enquiries.

Step one: find out what is available in your area

- The *Yellow Pages* lists local groups under 'crèche facilities and services', 'day nurseries' and 'nursery schools'.

- The Local Education Office (number from the phone book or library) should provide a list of state nursery schools.

- Local Social Services (early years section) should provide a list of all childminders, local playgroups and nurseries.

- Local libraries hold lists of groups, but you can't take the library list away with you!

- Your local schools may tell you which groups most of their children come from. This can be useful if you know that your child will be going to the local school at age five.

- Contact Parent helpline for details of childcare in your area on (0171) 837 5513 (10 a.m.–5 p.m.).

Step two: personal arrangements

Once you know all the types of childcare in your area you should consider:

- how many days and which days would be the most convenient for you and your child

- whether you would prefer mornings and/or afternoons

- the cost of the sessions and of travel to and from the group.

- Draw up a short list of three or four options which you think you would like to explore further.

Step three: knowing what to look for when you visit

- Make an informal visit first and notice what the group/childminder is like when they are not expecting you! Note your initial impressions, eg do they make you feel welcome? Do the children seem happy?

- If you like the group/childminder, arrange to return for a proper visit. Ask if they have any written information and are registered with the local authority.

- Try to make your main visit without your child so you are free to watch and listen without distraction. Arrive early to watch the children arriving and notice how they greet the staff/childminder. Are they pleased to be there?

- Ask if you can stay to watch quietly on your own for a few minutes. A good group/childminder should welcome this, but badly run childcare facilities can rarely keep the children happily occupied for long without problems showing, particularly if they only expected you to stay for a short while.

Checklist after visit to playgroup/childminder

Name of group　　　　　　　　　　　*Date of visit*

　1. Did you like the atmosphere of the group?　　　Yes/No
　2. Did the children seem happy?　　　　　　　　　Yes/No
　3. Were they well supervised?　　　　　　　　　　Yes/No
　4. Did they have a good range of activities?　　　Yes/No
　5. Would your child/children feel comfortable there?　Yes/No
　6. Can you afford the costs?　　　　　　　　　　　Yes/No
　7. Can your child have the sessions you want?　　Yes/No
　8. Are you totally happy with the group?　　　　　Yes/No

If you have 6 or more 'Yes' answers you should visit again taking your child with you. Watch his or her reaction and fill in the final section of the checklist.

　9. Did your child enjoy the visit?　　　　　　　　Yes/No
　10. Did he/she seem relaxed in the group/with the
　　　childminder?　　　　　　　　　　　　　　　　Yes/No
　11. Did the staff ask his/her name?　　　　　　　Yes/No
　12. Did you still like the group on this visit?　　Yes/No

Other comments:

Step four: making your decision

A particularly charming childminder or playgroup leader can leave you with good impressions, but try filling in the checklist on p. 104 after your visit.

Step five: checking that you made the right choice

After four to six weeks settling in, your child should look forward to going and talk about what they have done. That is the best indicator that you have made the right choice!

CONSIDERING THE BEST ALTERNATIVES

There are a range of options for you when it comes to choosing the best form of childcare for you and your child's needs. On pp. 106–109 is a useful guide that will help explore all the options.

ORGANISING AFTER-SCHOOL CHILDCARE

Childcare is often more difficult to organise for children of school age than for the under-fives. There aren't many jobs around where you can arrive at 9.30am after dropping the children off at school, leave at 2.45pm to take them home, and also not work during the school holidays and half-terms.

Kids' clubs have been developed for this reason. They often provide a safe place to play before school and two to three hours afterwards. They bridge the gap between school and working hours. There are over 1,500 clubs in the UK and there are plans to increase this to 3,000 with support from the government.

They are usually based in schools and use these facilities. Often the clubs pick up the children from school, and you only have to collect from the club when you've finished work or college.

Kids' Club Network is the national umbrella body for holiday playschemes and out-of-school play and care for children aged 5–12.

WORKING OUT THE COST IMPLICATIONS

Childcare costs can be a major outlay so it is important to consider the best options for you. Costs vary throughout the country, and sometimes even locally, as does choice and availability. Your own individual choice will be affected by the age of your children and your own needs and circumstances.

A Guide to Childcare

	Family and Friends	Child-minder	Mothers help	Nanny	Au pair
One person looking after your child	Yes	Yes	Yes	Yes	Yes
Staff/child ratio	1:1	1:3/4	1:1	1:1	1:1
Age range	Any age	0–5	Any age	Any age	Any age
Consistency of childcare	Probably	Long-term care	Tend to move on quite soon	Varies	Turnover high
Other children being cared for alongside	Family usually no; friends often have their own children too	Yes—ages mixed	No	No, but you could share with another family	No
Educational activities	Possibly	Possibly	Possibly	Possibly	Unlikely
Training/experience	Usually experience only	Usually experience only	Little	Usually trained; experience varies	No
Must be registered with local authority	No	Yes	No	No	No
Childcare in own home	Possibly	No	Yes	Yes	Yes
Have to take child	Possibly	Yes	No	No	No
Have to pick child up on time	Possibly	Yes	Less so if they live in	Less so if they live in	Less so
Help in your home	Possibly	No	Housework	Child-related home duties	Housework
Hours shorter than usual working day/ will need supplementing	No	No	No	No	Yes for pre-school children
Problems when your child is ill	Possibly	Probably if she cares for other children	Possibly inexperienced to look after	No	Inexperienced and hours too short

Day nursery	Workplace nursery/crêche	Playgroup/nursery class	After-school club
No	No	No	No
1:8 (3–5) 1:3 (0–2)	1:8	1:8	1:8
6 mths–5	2–5	3–5	5–15
Turnover of staff may be high		Likely	Likely
Yes	Yes	Yes	Yes
Probably	Probably	Yes	Usually no
Yes	Yes	Yes	At least half the staff
Yes	Yes	Yes	Usually, but not statutory
No	No	No	No
Yes	Yes	Yes	Normally will collect from shcool
Yes	Yes	Yes	Yes
No	No	No	No
No	No	Yes	Yes, 3 p.m.–6 p.m., except holidays

Not applicable, as child will not attend if ill

	Family and Friends	Child-minder	Mothers help	Nanny	Au pair
Problems when you are ill	Probably not	Getting child there	No	No	No
Problems when you child carer is ill	Yes	Yes	Yes	Possibly	Possibly
Care for children of school age after school	Yes	Possibly	Yes	Yes	Yes
School holiday cover	Yes	Yes	Yes	Yes	Yes
You can specify to your own child's needs	Yes	Possibly	Yes	Yes	Yes
Flexible hours to suit your particular needs	Possibly	Possibly	Yes	Yes	Yes (may need to go to college)
Cost	Low cost or pay in kind	Varies	Varies	Varies	Board plus a min. of £35 pw.
Where do you find childcare	By asking	List from local authority	Advertise/ agency	Advertise/ *Lady* magazine, nanny agency	Au pair agency

Can I get any help with costs?
A government scheme linked to Family Credit provides up to £60 towards childcare. Eligibility will depend on your level of income. Enquire at your local Benefits Agency or Jobcentre. There are often schemes targeted at lone parents, and some playgroups and kids' clubs have reduced rates. Ask your local Social Services department (under-eights department), who should have details of ways to assist towards childcare costs in your area.

GETTING SUPPORT AND ADVICE

It is important to explore all the options as sometimes your first and immediate choice cannot always suit your needs and there could be much better alternatives around the corner. Although childcare can be limited in some areas and with long waiting lists, many childcare organisations give priority to working lone parents.

The best source of local childcare information is the childcare

Day nursery	Workplace nursery/crèche	Playgroup/ nursery class	After-school club
You need to get children there and collected, need help at home			
No	No	No	No
No	No	No	Yes
If private, open all year. State nursery closed in holidays	May have fixed holidays	Same as school term	Usually special school holiday playscheme
No	No	No	No
No	No	No	No
Varies	Varies	Varies	Varies
List from local authority, *Yellow Pages*	Employer/trade union	List from local authority	School list from local authority, local education authority, Kids' Club Network

division (under-eights department) at your local Social Services, usually listed under the name of your local authority. The Citizens' Advice Bureau and the library should also have information.

Local single parent groups can be very beneficial in regard to providing support and information on childcare, and will give you an opportunity to meet others in the same position and perhaps help each other.

Gingerbread produce a guide, *Free to Work*, that lists all the childcare information services in the country.

DISCUSSION POINTS

1. Use the childcare guide (pp. 106–109) and tick the sources of childcare that could meet your needs.

2. Look through the Useful Addresses at the back of this book, and write or telephone to all the relevant sources. For example, if you

need a childminder, contact the National Association of Child-minders. Contact your Social Services for a local list of childcare.

3. Take the step-by-step guide (pp. 103–105) and check out local childcare.

11
Developing a Social Life and Enjoying Yourself

'I felt so isolated and lonely, and the more I longed to go out, the more difficult I found it when people invited me. I normally made excuses and then spent the whole evening regretting it.'

Developing a social life is very important, you need to have fun. If you're stuck at home, how on earth can you meet people? You need to ensure that you get out at least one night a week. It will be hard to organise, but in return you will find your energy renewed. Fig. 7 contains some suggestions.

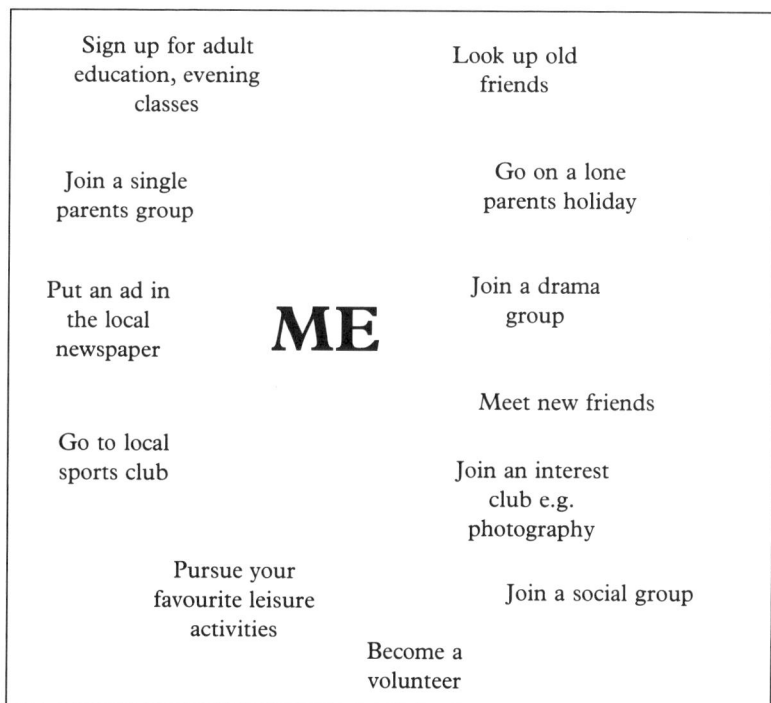

Sign up for adult education, evening classes

Look up old friends

Join a single parents group

Go on a lone parents holiday

Put an ad in the local newspaper

ME

Join a drama group

Meet new friends

Go to local sports club

Join an interest club e.g. photography

Pursue your favourite leisure activities

Join a social group

Become a volunteer

Fig. 7. Ideas for developing your social life.

GOING OUT

Going out, alone or with friends, is not easy, and a variety of reasons prevent you taking the steps to do something which is very important to you and your children. It is part of the process of 'giving time to yourself'. As a single parent you have the double dose of being the responsible parent and you need to let your hair down and sometimes be the child and go and play with your chosen playmates.

ARRANGING BABYSITTERS

Finding a babysitter and being able to pay them is a nightmare for all parents. It is a question of word of mouth amongst friends, putting ads in shop windows, contacting local single parent clubs, asking at your child's playgroup. Babysitting circles are a good idea for two parent families but often impractical for single parents—who is going to look after your kids when you are looking after someone else's? Is it easier for the kids to 'sleep over' at a friend's house? Think creatively—of opportunities rather than obstacles. Arranging a good source of evening childcare is essential if you want to Go Out!

MEETING NEW FRIENDS AND PARTNERS

Lone parenting can be very isolating and if you are suffering the effects of a split, you can find friends disappearing into the woodwork. You will benefit from making new friends and you could, if you wish, start on the road to meeting a new partner.

Rejection is a big fear when considering new friends or a new partner in your life. You may feel that you have been left once already, and starting all over again brings the fear of only going through the same. Remember the old cliché that you should not judge all people on the basis of what some have done to you. Often you are faced with the two extremes: one of total distrust, that 'they' are only going to do the same to you as the last one, or the other, a totally romantic illusion that the next partner will be wonderful.

These are all normal feelings of anticipation. Go easy, and have confidence in yourself.

If you are newly out of a relationship, try to see that relationship as like a death, and just as with a death it is necessary to grieve properly. You are not capable of making rational, logical, decisions about new partners in your life at this time, but you do need to *feel* again and have a good time.

You need to be sure any new friends and potential partners will not take away from your happiness, but will bring a happiness of their own.

INTRODUCING YOUR CHILDREN TO YOUR DATE

This can be a nightmare but don't be put off, just remember a few golden rules:

- You may be happy, but don't take it for granted that your children will share your enthusiasm for the new partner in your life.

- It takes children a long time to get over their loss of a parent, whether through death or splitting up. Just because you are 'over the moon' about someone doesn't mean your children will like them.

- The last thing your children want is someone to replace the 'absent' parent, and 'take away' their full-time parent from them.

- Let them make their own mind up and don't force them before they are ready.

- Arrange the initial meetings to be short but frequent, relaxed and informal.

- Be honest.

MANAGING A NEW RELATIONSHIP

Give any new relationship plenty of time. This is not easy as your children take up most of your hours and giving time to the new relationship could mean you have little left for yourself. Children can pressurise the relationship to move fast if they feel they will gain, so remember to keep control. If someone really cares for you they will give you the time you need. It is important to note that second relationships have a strong failure rate and the experience of living in a step-family can too often turn out to be short and distressing.

Case study: Pamela regrets a second relationship

Pamela was widowed at 30, and fell into another relationship quite quickly but it had disastrous consequences: 'When a new partner moved in the conflict became intolerable. It was horrible. He was jealous of my children and expected me to give all my attention to him. My eldest son realised he could cause an argument by getting me in the middle. There would be rows about everything, including what television channel they were watching. It was like having to choose between my lover or my children all the time. It might have been easier if he had tried to take to the children more, but it was not easy. There are bound to be difficulties when a new man comes in to look after someone else's children, particularly boys. You need a very special kind of person for that. I regret the experience. One day when Jason was cheeky he chased him up to the bathroom, broke down the door and wanted to hit him. At that point I realised it had to end. I jumped into the relationship because of severe loneliness and did not give myself and the kids proper time. I am now seeing someone who is happy to give me time and the boys like him.'

HAVING A SEX LIFE

The physical longing for someone to hold and caress you in an intimate way is part of the process of feeling alone and isolated. You should not confuse the need for sex (which is quite legitimate) with love, and not enter into a permanent relationship until you are very sure. Children often misunderstand seeing their parent in bed with someone, and often will relate this quickly to the other parent. It is best to be initially discreet, which is not easy. Above all, keep a good sense of humour.

GOING ON HOLIDAY

Holidays are important. Let's face it, we could all do with one. However, 40 per cent of people in the UK take no holiday in any given year. The biggest reason is that they cannot afford one, or that they prefer (or need) to spend their money on something else.

Stress, loneliness and overwhelming responsibilities are all too familiar to lone parents, especially those struggling on a low income. For such people, a holiday can make all the difference. There are a range of organisations that specialise in low cost holidays targeted at single parents (see the Useful Addresses section).

Case study: Sue enjoys single parent holiday clubs

'Holidaying alone with my children has often been a bad experience. It is a big responsibility and after coping with quarrelling, fighting, anxiety about them being a nuisance to other people, disappearances behind rocks or into shops, you go home feeling like you need another holiday. The advantage of going with a single parent club is that the children all play together so their parents can have some breathing space and the friendship of others in the same position. The club helps you broaden your horizons and visit places you would hesitate to go to on your own. My son was very quiet when we went to the station but suddenly said "I can't believe we're going on holiday. When I go back to school I can tell my friends I've been on holiday; just like them." It was a caravan holiday and the children loved it. The site had lots for the children to do—play areas, climbing frames, indoor and outdoor pools. I began to really enjoy myself as we met lots of single parents, although there was only one single parent dad amongst sixteen single mums!'

DISCUSSION POINTS

1. Explore all your options for finding a babysitter. Make up a list and discuss regular arrangements with them.

2. Find out about all the things you could do in your area by visiting your local tourist information office or the library. Make contact with local groups that interest you.

3. Write to all the holiday organisations listed in the Useful Addresses section.

12
Taking Pride in What You Achieve

'After years of struggling, and having many despairing moments, I am very proud of what I have done. I have three wonderful, lively and bright children, who love me as much as I love them. I once moaned about my situation to a female friend who is in her forties, divorced and has no children. She looked at me and said, "How can you sit there, and say your life is bad. Yes, I have my own house, and a well-paid job, but I don't have the love of children, and I would sacrifice everything for that." I thought about this and realised what I had and what I had achieved.'

You are doing a great job bringing up your children and you should be very proud of yourself. Being a parent is not easy. Being a lone parent is hard. You have to keep going when all you want to do is hide away under a stone. You have to continue against the odds as your children rely totally on you on a day-to-day basis. You become expert in making ends meet, and dodge one crisis after another. You learn to hold your head high when society cruelly criticises you. Many of you not only fulfil the incredibly important job of being a parent but also manage to go to college, hold down a job, or write books about being a single parent. You deserve a lot of praise.

The key to being a 'successful single parent' is to learn to be happy with yourself and think positively, even when you are facing a disaster. You have to believe that whatever you are facing, positive action can win the day. There is no magical wand to wave, and life will be hard. No easy solutions, but you can slowly, step by step, improve your situation and achieve your goals. It may take time, but they are achievable. Remember you have special people rooting for you, they are called your children.

BUILDING UP YOUR CONFIDENCE

You need to look to the future and plan. It is hard especially as the day-to-day involvement of children always makes planning very difficult. You need to build your confidence up and this takes time and effort. Remember that everyone suffers from doubts and uncertainties.

Confidence is about feeling OK with yourself, and learning to be proud of what you are achieving. To achieve better confidence, you need to:

● respect yourself

● take responsibility for yourself—for what you think, feel and do

● not see yourself purely in the role of mother, father or single parent, but as a person in your own right

● ask for what you want—don't expect other people to guess what you want

● respect other people and their rights.

You need to know what you want and want to say. Don't be afraid of how people may react as the worst they can do is only say 'no'.

Learn to deal with things as they arise. Don't put them off. For example, if you get a letter demanding payment, it is no good hiding it. Be honest. If you cannot pay, tell the person you owe the money to, or go and get advice. Don't let it linger. You will feel much better for this action, feel in control.

WRITING A PERSONAL ACTION PLAN

A person action plan will help you to:

● focus what you want for your future

● decide what action you need to take to achieve what you want

● think about the problems that you will need to resolve

● think about possible solutions to these problems

● plan in a way which will enable you to tackle problems and achieve what you want.

Use the outline on p. 118 to get you started.

Personal Action Plan

Date

Name

What I want to do

Action to be taken

Problems (what might stop me from taking these actions)

Solutions

When? (time scale)

Comments

THINKING ABOUT PROBLEMS AND SOLUTIONS

Problems *can* be resolved. That is what you have to believe, even when you can only feel total despair. You need to stop and think about your problems and put them into some order. What are your problems?

I have no home, and I'm living in bed and breakfast . . .

I cannot find decent childcare, and have to give up my job . . .

I have a large gas bill which I cannot pay . . .

My ex-partner is not paying any maintenance . . .

These are real and frightening situations faced by single parents, and there are no easy answers, but you will achieve nothing by wallowing in self-pity. You have to say 'Look, this can be resolved. There is a solution.'

The first step is to seek out help and get advice. This will enable you to think rationally about the problem and get a clear picture about the way to resolve it. If you are facing homelessness, you can ask your housing advice centre on all the local options, you can contact single parent support groups and ask what others have done. Often the situation is not as bad as your imagination makes it.

Case study: Sally loses her home

'I thought I was going to lose everything. I had tried to keep the house my ex and I had bought, but there were arrears and the building society was taking me to court for repossession. I felt lonely and rarely went out. I was afraid to ask the local council for help as I thought I would be put into bed and breakfast and I could not bear the thought of that. Out of desperation I wrote to an agony aunt in a magazine. I was surprised to get a quick reply. She told me to go to the local housing authority and explained my rights and gave me addresses of single parent support groups and pen pal clubs. The local authority got the building society to delay action for three months and nominated me to a housing association. I wrote to a pen pal club. Six months later I was in a house that was nearer to my family and better than the one I had before, at a rent which will enable me to make the steps back to work, and I have met some really good friends through the club.'

Sally's experience shows that even the simple act of writing a letter out of desperation can be a way to finding a positive solution. She took the advice and even though she lost her house, she found a new one that in fact improved her situation. No one can say it is easy. In fact it is hard, but only positive thought and action will improve your situation.

SEEKING SUPPORT AND PRACTICAL HELP

Throughout this book, you have been advised to seek advice and support in tackling important issues in your life. As a single parent you need and have a right to support and practical help, and it is readily available from a variety of sources.

It is always a good idea to seek out sources for support and advice when in fact you don't need it, then when you do you'll know exactly where to go. The two best local sources of information on what advice and support networks there are in your area are the library and Citizens' Advice Bureau. Both will have details of local support groups and of specialist advice whether debt counselling, housing or legal.

Gingerbread and Span are the two national umbrella organisations that support single parents, and both will be able to put you in touch with a group in your area. If it is too far for you to go, you'll find these organisations only too willing to help you link with others to form a more local group. Gingerbread has a national advice line which is always worth a ring. The National Council for One Parent Families is more a campaign organisation that provides information on all aspects of being a single parent and is constantly trying to improve our status in society. It is worth considering joining one of the above organisations purely for the positive information they provide.

There are a range of support groups emerging for single parent fathers, single parents with special needs, and gay lone parents. (See the Useful Addresses section.)

ENJOYING YOUR CHILDREN

It is not easy always to enjoy your children especially as you are chief cook and bottle-washer, cleaner, taxi driver, carer and provider, but the joy of being a parent is the children and you can get great support from them if you let them.

Start to smile and laugh. Break the routine up. Dinner does not have to be at a set time. You could have a picnic on the lounge floor in winter, or go for a walk and feed the ducks after school. Routines are good for children but occasionally breaking them will do wonders. Children love spontaneity and surprises. They also really love seeing their parent laugh and being happy. And it can be fun!

DISCUSSION POINTS

1. Write your personal action plan and set five key goals which you wish to achieve over the next year.

2. Discuss things that you enjoy doing with your children and things they enjoy doing with you, and plan a series of activities and trips.

3. Make a detailed list of all the local support and advice services in your area. Pin it up on the wall. Visit your local support group or perhaps establish one.

Appendix

On the following pages are reproduced two of the
forms you are most likely to encounter in legal
proceedings relating to your children.

Statement of Arrangements for Children
(Form M4, Appendix 1 FPR 1991)

FAMILY PROCEEDINGS RULES
Rule 2.2(2)

In the	County Court
Petitioner	
Respondent	
No. of Matter *(always quote this)*	

To the Petitioner

You must complete this form
if you or the respondent have any children   ●   under 16

                    or ●   over 16 but under 18 if they are at school
                                or college or are training for a trade,
                                profession or vocation.

Please use black ink.

Please complete Parts I, II and III.

Before you issue a petition for divorce try to reach agreement with your husband/wife over the proposals for the children's future. There is space for him/her to sign at the end of this form if agreement is reached.

If your husband/wife does not agree with the proposals he/she will have the opportunity at a later stage to state why he/she does not agree and will be able to make his/her own proposals.

You should take or send the completed form, signed by you (and, if agreement is reached, by your husband/wife) together with a copy to the Court when you issue your petition.

Please refer to the explanatory notes issued regarding completion of the prayer of the petition if you are asking the Court to make any order regarding the children.

The Court will only make an order if it considers that an order will be better for the child(ren) than no order.

If you wish to apply for any of the orders which may be available to you under Part I or II of the Children Act 1989 you are advised to see a solicitor.

You should obtain legal advice from a solicitor or, alternatively, from an advice agency. Addresses of solicitors and advice agencies can be obtained from the Yellow Pages and the Solicitors Regional Directory which can be found at Citizens Advice Bureaux, Law Centres and any local library.

To the Respondent

The petitioner has completed Parts I, II and III of this form
which will be sent to the Court at the same time that the divorce petition is filed.

Please read all parts of the form carefully.

If you agree with the arrangements and proposals for the children you should sign Part IV of the form.

Please use black ink. You should return the form to the petitioner, or his/her solicitor.

If you do not agree with all or some of the arrangements or proposals you will be given the opportunity of saying so when the divorce petition is served on you.

Part I – Details of the children

Please read the instructions for boxes 1, 2 and 3 before you complete this section

1. Children of both parties

(Give details only of any children born to you and the Respondent or adopted by you both)

	Forenames	Surnames	Date of birth
(i)			
(ii)			
(iii)			
(iv)			
(v)			

2. Other children of the family

(Give details of any other children treated by both of you as children of the family: for example your own or the Respondent's)

	Forenames	Surname	Date of birth	Relationship to Yourself	Respondent
(i)					
(ii)					
(iii)					
(iv)					
(v)					

3. Other children who are not children of the family

(Give details of any children born to you or the Respondent that have not been treated as children of the family or adopted by you both)

	Forenames	Surnames	Date of birth
(i)			
(ii)			
(iii)			
(iv)			
(v)			

Part II – Arrangements for the children of the family

This part of the form must be completed. Give details for each child if arrangements are different. If necessary, continue on another sheet and attach it to this form

4.	Home details *(Please tick the appropriate boxes)*	
	(a) The addresses at which the children now live	
	(b) Give details of the number of living rooms, bedrooms, etc. at the addresses in (a)	
	(c) Is the house rented or owned and by whom? Is the rent or any mortgage being regularly paid?	☐ No ☐ Yes
	(d) Give the names of all other persons living with the children including your husband/wife if he/she lives there. State their relationship to the children.	
	(e) Will there be any change in these arrangements?	☐ No ☐ Yes *(please give details)*

5.   Education and training details *(Please tick the appropriate boxes)*

(a) Give the names of the school, college or place of training attended by each child.

(b) Do the children have any special educational needs?

☐ No   ☐ Yes *(please give details)*

(c) Is the school, college or place of training, fee-paying?

☐ No   ☐ Yes *(please give details of how much the fees are per term/year)*

Are fees being regularly paid?

☐ No   ☐ Yes *(please give details)*

(d) Will there be any change in these arrangements?

☐ No   ☐ Yes *(please give details)*

6. Childcare details *(Please tick the appropriate boxes)*

(a) Which parent looks after the children from day to day? If responsibility is shared, please give details.	
(b) Does that parent go out to work?	☐ No ☐ Yes *(please give details of his/her hours of work)*
(c) Does someone look after the children when the parent is not there?	☐ No ☐ Yes *(please give details)*
(d) Who looks after the children during school holidays?	
(e) Will there be any change in these arrangements?	☐ No ☐ Yes *(please give details)*

7. Maintenance *(Please tick the appropriate boxes)*

(a) Does your husband/wife pay towards the upkeep of the children? If there is another source of maintenance, please specify.	☐ No ☐ Yes *(please give details of how much)*
(b) Is the payment made under a court order?	☐ No ☐ Yes *(please give details, including the name of the court and case number)*
(c) Is the payment following an assessment by the Child Support Agency?	☐ No ☐ Yes *(please give details of how much)*
(d) Has maintenance for the children been agreed?	☐ No ☐ Yes
(e) If not, will you be applying for: ● a child maintenance order from the court ● child support maintenance through the Child Support Agency?	☐ No ☐ Yes ☐ No ☐ Yes

5

8. | **Details for contact with the children** *(Please tick the appropriate boxes)*

(a) Do the children see your husband/wife?

☐ No   ☐ Yes *(please give details of how often and where)*

(b) Do the children ever stay with your husband/wife?

☐ No   ☐ Yes *(please give details of how much)*

(c) Will there be any change to these arrangements?

Please give details of the proposed arrangements for contact and residence.

☐ No   ☐ Yes *(please give details of how much)*

6

9.	Details of health *(Please tick the appropriate boxes)*	
	(a) Are the children generally in good health?	☐ Yes ☐ No *(please give details of any serious disability or chronic illness)*
	(b) Do the children have any special health needs?	☐ No ☐ Yes *(please give details of the care needed and how it is to be provided)*

10.	Details of care and other court proceedings *(Please tick the appropriate boxes)*	
	(a) Are the children in the care of a local authority, or under the supervision of a social worker or probation officer?	☐ No ☐ Yes *(please give details including any court proceedings)*
	(b) Are any of the children on the Child Protection Register?	☐ No ☐ Yes *(please give details of the local authority and the date of registration)*
	(c) Are there or have there been any proceedings in any Court involving the children, for example adoption, custody/residence, access/contact wardship, care, supervision or maintenance? (You need not include any Child Support Agency proceedings here).	☐ No ☐ Yes *(please give details and send a copy of any order to the Court)*

7

Part III — To the Petitioner

Conciliation

If you and your husband/wife do not agree about the arrangements for the child(ren), would you agree to discuss the matter with a Conciliator and your husband/wife?

☐ No   ☐ Yes

Declaration

I declare that the information I have given is correct and complete to the best of my knowledge.

Signed   (Petitioner)

Date:

Part IV — To the Respondent

I agree with the arrangements and proposals contained in Part I and II of this form.

Signed   (Respondent)

Date:

Application for an Order

(Children Act 1989)

Form C1

The Court	To be completed by the Court
	Date issued
The full name(s) of the child(ren)	
	Case number
	Child(ren)'s number(s)

1. **About you (the Applicant).**

   State • *your title, full name, address, telephone number, date of birth and relationship to each child above*
   • *your solicitor's name, address, reference, telephone, fax and DX numbers.*

2. **The child(ren) and the order(s) you are applying for.**

   For each child state • *the full name, date of birth and sex*
   • *the type of order(s) you are applying for (for example, residence order, contact order, supervision order).*

3. **Other cases which concern the child(ren).**

   If there have ever been, or there are pending, any court cases which concern
   - *a child whose name you have put in paragraph 2*
   - *a full, half or step brother or sister of a child whose name you have put in paragraph 2*
   - *a person in this case who is or has been, involved in caring for a child whose name you have put in paragraph 2,*

   please attach a copy of the relevant order and give
   - *the name of the Court*
   - *the name and **panel** address (if known) of the guardian ad litem, if appointed*
   - *the name and contact address (if known) of the court welfare officer, if appointed*
   - *the name and contact address (if known) of the solicitor appointed for the child(ren).*

4. **The Respondent(s).**

   (Appendix 3 Family Proceedings Courts Rules 1991; Schedule 2 Family Proceedings (Children Act 1989) Rules 1991).
   For each Respondent state • *the title, full name and address*
                                     • *the date of birth (if known) or the age*
                                     • *the relationship to each child.*

5. **Others to whom notice is to be given.**

    (Appendix 3 Family Proceedings Rules 1991, Schedule 2 Family Proceedings Courts (Children Act 1989) Rules 1991).

    For each person state
    - *the title, full name and address*
    - *the date of birth (if known) or age*
    - *the relationship to each child.*

6. **The care of the child(ren).**

    For each child in paragraph 2 state
    - *the child's current address and how long the child has lived there*
    - *whether it is the child's usual address and who cares for the child there*
    - *the child's relationship to the other children (if any).*

7. **Social Services.**

    For each child in paragraph 2 state
    - *whether the child is known to the Social Services. If so, give the name of the social worker and the address of the Social Services Department*
    - *whether the child is, or has been, on the Child Protection Register. If so, give the date of registration.*

3

8. **The education and health of the child(ren).**

For each child state
- *the name of the school, college or place of training which the child attends*
- *whether the child is in good health. Give details of any serious disabilities or ill health*
- *whether the child has any special needs.*

9. **The Parent(s) of the child(ren).**

For each child state
- *the full name of the child's mother and father*
- *whether the parents are, or have been, married to each other*
- *whether the parents live together. If so, where*
- *whether, to your knowledge, either of the parents have been involved in a Court case concerning a child. If so, give the date and the name of the Court.*

10. **The Family of the child(ren) (other children).**

For any other child not already mentioned in the family (for example, a brother or a half sister) state
- *the full name and address*
- *the date of birth (if known) or age*
- *the relationship of the child to you.*

11. **Other adults.**

State • *the full name, of any other adults (for example, lodgers) who live at the same address as any child named in paragraph 2*
       • *whether they live there all the time*
       • *whether, to your knowledge, the adult has been involved in a Court case concerning a child. If so, give the date and the name of the Court.*

12. **Your reason(s) for applying and any plans for the child(ren).**

State briefly your reasons for applying and what you want the Court to order.
• *Do not give a full statement if you are applying for an order under Section 8 of Children Act 1989. You may be asked to provide a full statement later.*
• *Do not complete this section if this form is accompanied by a prescribed supplement.*

13. **At the Court.**

State • *whether you will need an interpreter at Court (parties are responsible for providing their own). If so, please specify the language*
       • *whether disabled facilities will be needed at Court.*

Signed
(Applicant)   Date

Useful Addresses

GENERAL ADVICE

Citizens' Advice Bureaux (CABx), 115–123 Pentonville Rd, London N1 9LZ. Tel: (0171) 833 2181. Details of your local CAB can be found in the telephone directory or by phoning the national office. CABx can help with a wide range of problems and may hold legal sessions and provide debt counselling.

Federation of Independent Advice Centres (FIAC), 13 Stockwell Rd, London SW9 9AU. Tel: (0171) 274 1893. FIAC is a network of advice centres around the country.

LONE PARENT ORGANISATIONS/GROUPS

Gingerbread, 16–17 Clerkenwell Close, London EC1R 0AA. Tel: (0171) 336 8183. Advice line: (0171) 336 8184. Gingerbread is the nationally recognised self-help association for one parent families. There are about 400 local groups operating in the UK and they meet regularly to provide mutual support and help for members and their children. Many groups also run a range of social activities.

Gingerbread Northern Ireland, 169 University Street, Belfast BT7 1HR. Tel: (01232) 231147.

Gingerbread Scotland, Maryhill Community Hall, 304 Maryhill Road, Glasgow G20 7YE. Tel: (0141) 353 0989.

Gingerbread Wales, 16 Albion Chambers, Cambrian Place, Swansea SA1 1RN. Tel: (01792) 648728.

National Council for One Parent Families, 255 Kentish Town Road, London NW5 2LX. Tel: (0171) 267 1361. Offers information for lone parents on welfare benefits, housing, divorce, maintenance, legal matters and bereavement.

Single Parent Action Network (SPAN), Millpond, Lower Ashley Road, Easton, Bristol BS5 0YJ. Tel: (0117) 951 4231. SPAN is a nationwide network of self-help organisations for single parents.

It is particularly concerned with poverty, racism and women's issues and can help new groups.

Scottish Council for Single Parents, 13 Gayfield Square, Edinburgh EH1 3AX. Tel: (0131) 556 3899.

One Plus, 39 Hope Street, Glasgow G2 6AE. Tel: (0141) 221 7150. Advice and information for lone parents in Scotland.

Single parent fathers

All the above groups include single parent dads. However, there are groups around the UK that cater for the particular needs of fathers bringing up their children alone:

Single Dads Support, 3 Oregan Close, New Malden, Surrey. Send SAE for information.

Fatherhood Support Group, The Old Library, New Street, Dawley, Telford, Shropshire. Tel: (01952) 501272.

BENEFITS

Income Support

Department of Social Security. Visit your local office or ring Freeline 0800 666 555. The address and telephone number of your local office should be in the *Yellow Pages* under 'government departments'.

DSS Benefit free advice lines:

Benefit enquiry line: 0800 666555.

Disability benefits: 0800 882200.

Family Credit

Family Credit Unit, DSS, Government Buildings, Warbreck Hill, Blackpool FY2 0YE. Family Credit Helpline Tel: (01253) 500 050. Free line: 0800 500222.

Child Benefit and One Parent Benefit

Child Benefit Centre, DSS Washington, Newcastle Upon Tyne NE88 1AA.

Housing and Council Tax Benefit

Local authority (council). The address and telephone number should be in the *Yellow Pages* under 'local government'. If you telephone, the switchboard should put you in touch with the department you need, eg housing, housing benefits, council tax.

General

The Child Poverty Action Group, 1–5 Bath Street, London EC1V 9PY. Tel: (0171) 253 3406. Produces a range of material including *The National Welfare Benefits Handbook.*

BEREAVEMENT

Cruse Bereavement Care, Cruse House, 26 Sheen Road, Richmond TW9 1UR. Tel: (0181) 940 4818. Helpline Tel: (0181) 322 7227 (9.30a.m.–5p.m. Mon–Fri). Has support groups around the country for the bereaved.

Bereavement Trust, Stanford Hall, Loughborough, Leicestershire LE12 5QR. Tel: (0509) 852333. Provides information about bereavement support services across the country.

Foundation for Black Bereaved Families, 11 Kingston Square, Salters Hill, London SE19 1JE. Tel: (0181) 661 7228. Provides support and advice to bereaved black families across the country.

The Gay Bereavement Project, c/o Gay Switchboard. Tel: (0171) 837 8324 (24 hours). Based in London, but can offer contacts for other parts of the country.

Institute of Family Therapy, 43 New Cavendish Street, London W1M 7RG. The Elizabeth Raven Memorial Fund offers free counselling to newly bereaved families or those with terminally ill family members.

National Association of Bereaved Services, 668 Charlton Street, London NW11 1JR. Tel: (0181) 388 2153. Provides a national network of support groups for the bereaved and can put you in touch with services in your area.

National Association of Widows/Widows Advisory Trust, 54–57 Allison Street, Digbeth, Birmingham B5 5TH. Tel: (0121) 643 8348.

CHILDCARE

Kids' Club Network, 279–281 Whitechapel Road, London E1 1BY. Tel: (0171) 247 3009. Gives advice and information on all aspects of out-of-school childcare. KCN is the national umbrella body for holiday playschemes and out-of-school play and care for children aged 5 to 12.

The Parent Helpline. Tel: (0171) 837 5513 (10 a.m.–5 p.m.). National helpline which gives parents details of childcare in their area.

Daycare Trust/National Childcare Campaign, Wesley House, 4 Wild Court, London WC2B 4AU. Tel: (0171) 405 5617.

National Childminding Association, 8 Mason Hill, Bromley, Kent BR2 9EY. Tel: (0181) 464 6164.

The National Early Years Network, 77 Holloway Road, London N7 8JZ. Tel: (0171) 607 9573. Provides details of local under-eight services.

National Association of Toy and Leisure Libraries, 68 Churchway, London NW1 1LT. Provides information about local toy libraries.

Pre-School Learning Alliance, 61/63 Kings Cross Road, London WC1X 9LL. Tel: (0171) 833 0991. Umbrella organisation for all the voluntary run playgroups in the UK.

CHILDREN

Childline, Freepost 1111, London N1 0BR. Tel: 0800 1111. Free counselling service for children. Available 24 hours a day.

Family Rights Group, The Print House, 18 Ashwin Street, London E8 3DL. Tel: (0171) 249 0008. Gives practical and legal advice to families, particularly for parents with children who may go into or are in local authority care.

National Children's Bureau, 8 Wakeley Street, London EC1V 7QE. Tel: (0171) 843 6000.

Cry-sis, BM Cry-sis, London WC1N 3XX. Tel: (0171) 404 5011. Self-help and support for families with excessively crying, sleepless and demanding children.

NSPCC (National Society for the Prevention of Cruelty to Children), 42 Curton Rd, London CC2A 3NH. Tel: (0171) 825 2500. Can be contacted for information and advice relating to the welfare of children.

CONTACTS

Singlescape, 18 Woolvestone Close, Suffolk IP2 9RY. Singlescape is the largest postal support and self-help pen-friend group of its kind in the UK with over 2,000 members. Send SAE.

National Federation of Solo Clubs, Room 8, Ruskin Chambers, 191 Corporation Street, Birmingham B4 6RY. Tel: (0121) 236 2879. Has 100 local branches throughout UK and is open to all single, widowed, divorced and separated people between 25 and 65 years old.

Cascade, Tardis Towers, New Inn, Pontypool, Gwent NP4 0LU. Tel: (01495) 755309. Social group (30–55 age group) with members throughout UK.

National Women's Register, 9 Bank Plain, Norwich NR2 4SL. Tel: (01603) 765392. Provides the chance to meet with other women locally for support and stimulation.

National Federation of 18 plus Groups, Head Office, Nicholson House, Old Court Road, Newent, Gloucestershire GL18 1AG. Provides a wide range of activities for young people aged 18–30, single or unattached, in 200 groups throughout UK.

COUNSELLING

Your GP may be able to offer counselling or refer you for counselling.

Relate—Marriage Guidance, Herbert Gray College, Little Church Street, Rugby, Warwickshire CV21 3AP. Has local branches around the country. Can be used by married or unmarried couples.

Samaritans: for details of local groups see the telephone directory or telephone (01753) 532713.

British Association for Counselling, 1 Regent Place, Rugby CV21 2PJ. Tel: (01788) 578328.

DEBT

National Debtline, 318 Summer Lane, Birmingham B19 3RL. Tel: (0121) 359 8501. Offers specialist debt advice and support.

Creditcure Voluntary Association, 109 Bramford Road, Ipswich IP1 2LP. Produces a newsletter and a debt survival manual. Send SAE.

(See also Citizens' Advice Bureaux, p. 136.)

DISABILITY/SPECIAL NEEDS

Citizen Advocacy Information and Training (CAIT), Unit 2K, Leroy House, 436 Essex Road, London N1 3QP. Tel: (0171) 359 8289. Information about advocacy services which help people with disabilities to deal with officials.

Contact-a-family, 70 Tottenham Court Road, London W1PP 0HA. Helpline: (0171) 383 3555. National charity providing information and support for parents of children with special needs.

Disability Alliance (ERA), 1st floor East, Universal House, 88–94 Wentworth Street, London E1 7SA. Tel: (0171) 247 8776. Provides information and advice by telephone and letter to people with disabilities and their carers.

Parentability, c/o National Childbirth Trust, Alexander House, Oldham Terrace, London W3 6NH. Tel: (0181) 653 7430.

Provides advice and has details of support groups and resources for parents with disabilities.

DOMESTIC VIOLENCE

Women's Aid Federation (England), PO Box 391, Bristol BS99 7WS. National Helpline: (0117) 963 3542. Has details of women's refuges around the country.

Northern Ireland Women's Aid, 129 University Street, Belfast BT7 1HP. Tel: (01232) 249041.

Scottish Women's Aid, 13/19 North Bank Street, The Mound, Edinburgh EH1 2LP. Tel: (0131) 221 0401.

Welsh Women's Aid, 38–48 Crwys Road, Cardiff CF2 4NN. Tel: (01222) 390874.

Southall Black Sisters, 52 Norwood Road, Southall UB2 4DW. Tel: (0181) 571 9595. Counselling and advice for Asian and black women experiencing domestic violence. Their advice also covers immigration, housing and matrimonial questions.

EMPLOYMENT

Careers and Occupational Information Centre (COIC), Moorfoot, Sheffield S1 4PQ. Tel: (01142) 753275.

Parents at Work, 77 Holloway Road, London N7 8JZ. Tel: (0171) 700 0281. Provides information on working parent support groups in the UK and all aspects of working combined with caring for children.

New Ways to Work, 309 Upper Street, London N1 2TY. Tel: (0171) 226 4026. Publishes booklets and fact sheets on all aspects of job sharing. Enquiries: Tuesdays (10 a.m.–1 p.m.), Wednesdays (12–3 p.m).

Women Returners Network, 8 John Adam Street, London WC2N 6EZ. Tel: (0171) 839 8188. Provides information about courses to update you; self-assessment and career planning.

Ownbase, 68 First Avenue, Bush Hill Park, Enfield, Middlesex EN1 1BN. A national network and newsletter for people who work from home.

ETHNIC MINORITIES

See Southall Black Sisters under Domestic Violence above.

FAMILY

National Stepfamily Association, 72 Willesden Lane, London NW6 7TA. Tel: (0171) 372 0844 (office); (0171) 372 0846 (counselling). Provides advice, support and information to stepfamilies; confidential telephone counselling service, newsletters and local support groups.

The Family Welfare Association, 501–505 Kingsland Road, London E8 4AU. Tel: (0171) 254 6251. Provides social work and social care services to families and individuals. A variety of services to people facing social and emotional difficulties, including family and relationship problems, bereavement, loneliness, poverty, unemployment and homelessness.

FURTHER EDUCATION

Further Education Unit, Unit 3, Citadel Place, Tinworth Street, London SE11 5EH. Tel: (0171) 962 1280. Will send you leaflets on further and higher education around the country.

Educational Guidance for Adults, PO Box 109, Hatfield Polytechnic, Hatfield, Herts. This is a free service. You get a one-hour interview after which advice is given on which further and higher education courses would suit you and where you can find them.

The Open College, FREEPOST TK1006, Brentford, Middlesex TW8 8BR. Freephone: 0800 300 760. Provides open learning courses with an emphasis on retraining and updating skills.

Open University (OU), Enquiry office, PO Box 71, Milton Keynes MK7 6AG. Tel: (01908) 274066. Offers a wide range of degree, non-degree and vocational courses.

The Council for the Accreditation of Correspondence Colleges, 27 Marylebone Road, London NW1 5JS. Tel: (0171) 935 5391.

National Extension College, 18 Brooklands Avenue, Cambridge CB2 2HN. Tel: (01223) 316644. Offers correspondence courses on a wide range of subjects.

HEALTH

Health Information Service. Tel: 0800 665544. Free confidential information service dealing with individual health enquiries and offering facts and advice on health services in your region.

MIND (National Association for Mental Health), Granta House, 15–19 Broadway, Stratford, London E15 4BQ. Tel: (0181) 519

2122. Provides information about the range of health problems and has leaflets about treatment and therapies. It also gives legal advice. Local MIND groups offer different services such as drop-in centres, counselling, referral to counsellors.

HOUSING

Housing Advice Centres: find details of your local advice centre by looking in the telephone directory or phone Shelter:
Shelter (National Campaign for Homeless People), 88 Old Street, London EC1V 9HU. Tel: (0171) 373 7841. Nightline 0800 446441.

HOLIDAYS FOR LONE PARENTS

Holiday Care Service, 2 Old Bank Chambers, Stations Road, Horley, Surrey RH6 9HW. Tel: (01293) 774535. Provides information on a range of specialist holidays and agencies. Produces a guide to holidays for one parent families.
HELP (Holiday Endeavour for Lone Parents), 29 The Crescent, Woodlands, Doncaster, South Yorkshire DN6 7PE. Tel: (01302) 725315.
HOP (Holidays for One Parent families), 51 Hampshire Road, Droysden, Manchester M43 7PH. Tel: (0161) 370 0337.
Single Parent Travel Club, 37 Sunningdale Park, Queen Victoria Road, New Tupton, Chesterfield. Tel: (01246) 865069.
One Parent Family Holidays, Kilonian Courtyard, Barrhill, Girvan, South Ayrshire KA26 0PS. Tel: (01465) 82288.
Splash, 19 North Street, Plymouth PL4 9AH. Tel: (01752) 674067.

IMMIGRATION/NATIONALITY

Joint Council for the Welfare of Immigrants, 115 Old Street, London EC1V 9JR. Tel: (0171) 251 8706. Specialist advice service on immigration and nationality problems.

LEGAL

Children's Legal Centre, c/o University of Essex, Winehoe Park, Colchester CO4 3SQ. Tel: (01206) 872562. Advice line: (01206) 873820 (2–5 p.m. Mon–Fri). Provides advice on young people and the law.
Disability Law Service, 116 Princeton Street, London WC1R 4BB. Tel: (0171) 831 8031/7740. A free service for people with disabili-

ties and their families, providing advice and some representation on all aspects of the law.

Gay and Lesbian Legal Advice (GLAD). Tel: (0171) 253 2043. A free phone line open in the evenings, providing free legal advice and referral to solicitors.

Law Centres Federation, Duchess House, 18–19 Warren Street, London W1P 5DB. Tel: (0171) 387 8570. Will give you details of your local law centre which can offer free legal advice and representation on specific issues.

Legal Aid Head Office, 85 Grays Inn Road, London WC1X 8AA. Tel: (0171) 813 1000.

Rights of Women, 52–54 Featherstone Street, London EC1Y 8RT. Tel: (0171) 251 6577. Free legal advice by telephone for women.

Solicitors Family Law Association (SFLA), PO Box 302, Orpington, Kent BR6 8QX. Tel: (01689) 850227. An association of solicitors specialising in family law. Send a stamped addressed envelope for a list of local solicitor members.

LESBIAN AND GAY

Lesbian Custody Project, c/o Rights of Women, 52–54 Featherstone Street, London EC1Y 8RT. Tel: (0171) 251 6577.

Lesbian and Gay switchboard, Tel: (0171) 837 7324. Can provide details of local lesbian and gay support groups and switchboards.

MAINTENANCE

Child Support Agency, Millbank Tower, 21–24 Millbank, London SW1 4QU. Public enquiry line: (0345) 133133. General advice on any aspect of child maintenance.

MEDIATION

National Family Mediation service (NFM), Charitybase, The Chandlery, 50 Westminster Bridge Rd, London SE1 7QY. Tel: (0171) 721 7658. Can put you in touch with a local service, where you can receive mediation help. Some charge a fee for mediation sessions, while others are free. You may get help with fees under the Legal Aid scheme.

Family and Divorce Centre, 162 Tennison Rd, Cambridge CB1 2DP. Tel: (01223) 460136. Providing a range of services from legal advice to mediation and conciliation for people seeking divorce.

Family Mediators Association, The Old House, Rectory Gardens, Henbury, Bristol BS10 7AQ. Tel: (0117) 950 0140.

Family Mediation (Northern Ireland), 76 Dublin Road, Belfast BT2 7HP. Tel: (0232) 322914.

Family Mediation (Scotland), 127 Rose Street, South Lane, Edinburgh EH2 5BB. Tel: (0131) 220 1610.

Family Mediation (Wales), 33 Westgate Street, Cardiff, South Glamorgan CF1 1JE. Tel: (01222) 229692.

National Family Mediation, 9 Tavistock Place, London WC1H 9SN. Tel: (0171) 383 5993. Has details of mediation services around the country.

Divorce Conciliation and Advisory Service (DCAS), 38 Ebury Street, London SW1W 0LU. Tel: (0171) 730 2422.

PARENTING

Exploring Parenthood, Latimer Educational Centre, 194 Freston Road, London W10 6TT. Tel: (0181) 960 1678. A free national telephone advice line providing advice and counselling for parents. Also runs the Moyenda Project for black and Asian parents.

Home-start, Head Office, 2 Salisbury Rd, Leicester LE1 7QR. Tel: (01166) 255 4988. Has local schemes which offer regular support, friendship and practical help to families with at least one child under five. Volunteers visit families in their own homes. Details of local groups can be found in the local telephone directory or by contacting the head office.

Parentline: has a national network of telephone lines that offer help to parents who are having difficulties with parenting. Details can be found in the local telephone directory or by phoning (01449) 677707.

Step-family, 72 Willesden Lane, London NW6 7TA. Tel: (0171) 372 0844. (0171) 372 0846 (counselling).

Meet-A-Mum Association, 14 Willis Road, Croydon, Surrey CR0 2XX. Tel: (0181) 665 0357. Support and help for women suffering from post-natal depression, feeling isolated and tired after having a baby or just in need of a friend to share problems. Local groups and one-to-one contact.

Parents Anonymous. Tel: (0171) 263 8918 or (0181) 689 3136. A telephone helpline for all parents under stress.

Twin and Multiple Births Association, 54 Parkway, Exeter, Devon EX2 9NF. Tel: (01392) 431605.

Association of Shared Parenting, PO Box 2000, Dudley, West

Midlands DY1 1Y2. Promotes the child's right to the nurture of both parents after separation or divorce and encourages and supports parents in fulfilment of this right.

Parent Network, 44–46 Caversham Road, London NW5 2DS. Has groups throughout UK and provides training and practical help on all aspects of parenting.

PREGNANCY ADVICE AND COUNSELLING

British Pregnancy Advisory Service (BPAS), Austy Manor, Wooton Waven, Solihull B95 6BX.

Brook Advisory Centres, 153a East Street, London SE17 2SD. Tel: (0171) 240 0953.

RELATIONSHIPS

Relate, Herbert Grey College, Little Church Street, Rugby CV21 3AP. Tel: (01788) 73241. Confidential counselling on relationship problems of any kind.

Marriage Guidance (Scotland), 105 Hanover Street, Edinburgh EH2 1DG. Tel: (0131) 225 5006.

Families Need Fathers. Tel: (0171) 613 5060. Mainly concerned with helping children to maintain relationships with both parents following divorce or separation. They also advise and support parents and have a national network of voluntary contacts.

National Council for the Divorced and Separated, 13 High Street, Little Shelford, Cambridge CB2 5ES. Tel: (0116) 270595. Offers advice and the chance to meet others who are or have been through similar experiences.

Divorce Conciliation and Advisory Service (DCAS), 38 Ebury Street, London SW1W 0LU. Tel: (0171) 730 2422. Help and advice for parents to maintain workable arrangements of joint care for their children.

Both Parents Forever, 39 Clonmore Ave, Orpington, Kent BR6 9LE. Tel: (01689) 854343. Promotes the rights of grandparents, parents and children. Helps trace and return children in child abduction cases.

Catholic Marriage Advisory Council, Clitherow House, 1 Blythe Mew, Blythe Road, London W14 0NW. Tel: (0171) 371 1341.

WOMEN

National Alliance of Women's Organisations, 279–281 Whitechapel
Road, London E1 1BY. Tel: (0171) 247 70052.

VOLUNTEERING

National Association of Volunteer Bureaux, St Peters College, College
Road, Saltley, Birmingham B8 3TE. Tel: (0121) 327 0265. Will
put you in touch with your local bureau. You can also look in your
local telephone directory or ask at your local library.

Further Reading

SINGLE PARENT ISSUES

The Single Parents Survival Guide—How To Go It Alone Successfully (Caroline Buchanan and Sandra Sedgbeer).
One Parent Families (Sue Watkins, Crowood Press).
One Parent Plus—A Handbook for Single Parents (Jane Ward, Optima).
Just Me and the Kids—A Manual for Lone Parents (Gingerbread/ Bedford Square Press).
Soul Providers (ed. Gil McNeil, Virago Press). Eighteen lone parents give their personal view of life as a single parent.
Single and Pregnant (NCOPF).
How to Help: a Guide for Family and Friends of Lone Parents (NCOPF).

BENEFITS

National Welfare Benefits Handbook & Rights Guide to Non Means Tested Benefits (Child Poverty Action Group).
How to Claim State Benefits (Martin Rathfelder, How To Books).

BEREAVEMENT

Bereavement (Christopher Golding, Crowood Press). The practical aspects of bereavement.
What To Do When Someone Dies (Paul Harris, *Which*? Consumer Guide, distributed by Penguin Group). How to deal with the practical arrangements that have to be made after death.
Dealing with a Death in the Family (Sylvia Greenland, How To Books).

CHILDCARE

Free to Work—Comprehensive Guide to Childcare in England and Wales (Gingerbread).
What's on Where? The National Guide to School Age Childcare (Kids' Club Network).

CHILDREN

Helping Children Cope with Divorce (Rosemary Wells, Sheldon Press).
Helping Children Cope with Grief (Rosemary Wells, Sheldon Press).
Facing Grief—Bereavement and the Young Adult (Susan Wallbank, Lutterworth Press). One of the few books around written specifically for young people, this has particularly good sections on the different effects of a mother's or a father's death.

CHILDREN'S BOOKS ON FAMILY CHANGES

The following are children's books that tackle issues of family break-up, divorce, bereavement, and living in single parent families.
Children Don't Divorce (Rosemary Stones, Dinosaur Talk It Over Series).
You can be Spurs (Chris Ashley, Walker).
Mike's Lonely Summer (Caroline Nystrom, Lion).
Dad And Me series (Walker).
Finish the Story, Dad (Nicola Smee, Walker).
Emma's Monster (Marjorie Darke, Walkert).
Crazy Christmas (Jeanne Bettancourt, Pan Macmillan).
The Haunted Sand (Hugh Scott, Walker).
Worlds Apart (Jill Murphy, Walker).
Anna Magdalena—The Little Girl with the Big Name (Lion).
Grief in Children (Atle Dyregov, Jessica Kingsley).
How it Feels When a Parent Dies (ed. J. Krementz, Gollancz). Accounts by eighteen children of different ages of how they experienced a parent's death.
I Never Told Her I Loved Her (Sandra Chick, Livewire Books). A novel about a teenager coping with her mother's death and her new role as 'woman of the house'.
The Secret Garden (Frances Hodgson Burnett, Puffin). Classic children's book about two bereaved children finding friendship and renewed faith in life.

CUSTODY

Arrangements for Children in the Family (NCOPF).

CONTACTS

Future Friends Magazine. UK's leading independent magazine for single and unattached people. Available from Future Friends Magazine, PO Box 4, Goring-on Thames RG8 9DN.

Singles Review. A handbook of options for single people wishing to meet others in the UK. Bloodworth Press, Avondale Workshops, Woodland Way, Bristol BS15 1QH.

DEBT

Debt Advice Handbook (Mike Woolfe and Jill Ivison, CPAG).
Debt—A Survival Guide (Office of Fair Trading).

DIVORCE/RELATIONSHIP BREAK-UP

The Relate Guide to Starting Again (Sarah Litvinoff, Vermillion). A guide to the emotional aspects of dealing with a separation and how to help your children.

Divorced Parenting (Dr Soc Goldstein).

The Which? Guide to Divorce (Helen Garlick).

Going it Alone—Two Guides for Married and Unmarried Women (SHAC. Tel: (0171) 404 6929).

How to Survive Divorce (Roy Van de Brink-Budgen, How To Books).

DOMESTIC VIOLENCE

Domestic Violence—Don't Stand for it (Home Office).

EMPLOYMENT

Lone Parents Guide to Employment (National Council for One Parent Families/Child Support Agency). Available from Child Support Agency. Tel: (0345) 830830.

Working Mother—A Practical Handbook for Women Working or Wishing to Return to Work (Marianne Velmans and Sarah Litvinoff, Pocket Books).

Returning to Work—A Guide for Lone Parents (National Council for One Parent Families).

FAMILY

Families and How to Survive Them (Robin Skynner and John Cleese, Mandarin Paperbacks). An invaluable read for anyone wanting to understand how relationships within families have implications for the rest of our life.

HOLIDAYS

Holidays for One Parent Families (National Council for One Parent Families).
The Parent Guide—Children's Holidays (Kupperand).

HOUSING

Shelter Housing Rights Guide.

LAW

When Parents Separate—a Handbook of Law and Practice (Children's Legal Centre).

MAINTENANCE

A Guide to Child Support Maintenance (Child Support Agency).
Maintenance and the Child Support Agency (NCOPF).
For Parents who Live Apart (Child Support Agency).

TAX

A Guide for One Parent Families (available from your local Inland Revenue office).

WORKING FROM HOME

Working from Home (Marianne Gray, Piakus Books).
Working from Home (Ian Phillipson, How To Books, 2nd edition).

Glossary

Absent parent. A term introduced by the Child Support Act 1991. Refers to the parent who does not have day-to-day care of the child, as opposed to the **parent with care**.

Access. New word for '**contact**', used in Children Act 1989.

Adultery. Legal term used to describe sexual intercourse by a husband or wife with a third party (of the opposite sex) at any time before a decree absolute of divorce. You could have been separated from your married partner for some time, and yet still technically commit adultery, even though in your eyes the marriage relationship is over. In law the marriage is only over when a decree absolute is given by the courts.

Affidavit. A statement whose contents are sworn to be true. Used in legal procedures as a way of substantiating your claims or in answer to another's claims against you.

Au pair. Usually a young girl (18–25) learning language in a foreign country, providing childcare in return for accommodation, food and a small allowance.

Benefits. Financial assistance provided by the government, whether through the Department of Social Security/Benefits Agency (income support, family credit, etc) or through your local authority (housing and council tax benefit).

Bereavement. The state and sense of loss of a loved one.

Carer. A person who looks after the day-to-day welfare of others. A parent is a carer of his or her children.

Child Support Agency (CSA. The national body that deals with seeking **maintenance** from the absent parent. Part of the Department of Social Security.

Childcare. Care and oversight of a child. Usually a general reference to the arrangements for a child other than being cared for by parents or school. An additional service provided by other family members, friends, childminders, nannies, au pairs, playgroups, after-school clubs and nurseries.

Cohabitation. A couple living together as husband and wife with the implication that they are not married.

Conciliation. The service provided by a number of organisations to mediate between couples on matters which arise during separation and divorce. Some conciliation schemes are run in association with the courts, and some are run by voluntary organisations. (See also **mediation**.)

Contact. A contact order is one which enables a child literally to have some contact with the person in the order (usually the absent parent). Such contact could include visiting, staying overnight, sending and receiving letters, and so on.

Counselling. The service offered by a number of organisations, such as Relate, to anyone experiencing difficulties. Counsellors do not seek to give you the answers to your problems but to enable you to find the answers yourself through full and open discussion.

Creditors. People or organisations to whom you owe money. Could include shops, banks, building society, electricity board etc.

Custody. Traditional term used to describe which parent had the full responsibility of the child/children. The Children Act 1989 has changed towards giving every parent **parental responsibility** and in legal terms the word 'custody' has been replaced.

Debt. Money that you owe.

Decree absolute. Order dissolving a marriage.

Decree nisi. Document issued once the court is satisfied that the grounds for divorce are established, allowing the **petitioner** to apply to have the decree made absolute after a further six weeks and one day.

Ex-partner. Partner is a common term used for husband, wife, whether married or unmarried, but generally used when people are not married. 'Ex' refers to former partner, husband or wife.

Gay parenting. Term used to describe a parent who has had children normally through intercourse with the opposite sex, but whose sexual orientation means they wish to have relationships with their own sex. It does not impede in any way on their skills as a parent.

Green form. (See **Legal Aid**.)

Infidelity. When a lover or partner is unfaithful by having sexual intercourse with another.

Legal Aid. Government-funded scheme administered by Legal Aid Board based on financial eligiblity and merits of case. Anyone in need of legal help is entitled to apply for Legal Aid (using what is usually termed the Green Form).

Maintenance. Payments made to an **ex-partner**, usually to help towards the living costs of that person and/or the children of the couple.

Mediation. Refers to the method of getting couples to discuss a full range of issues which arise as a result of separation and divorce. Includes a discussion on arrangements for the children, financial and property matters. It has a broader focus than **conciliation** but basically means the same.

Parent with care. A term introduced by the Child Support Act 1991. Refers to the parent who has the day-to-day care of the child, as opposed to the **absent parent**.

Parental responsibility. A term introduced by the Children Act 1989. Refers to the rights, duties, powers, responsibilities and authority which a parent has in relation to a child. Mothers and married fathers have this responsibility automatically. Other people, including unmarried fathers, can also acquire it through the courts.

Partner. Term used to describe a live-in lover, husband, wife.

Pen Pal Club. A club that links like-minded people through writing letters.

Petitioner. The spouse (husband or wife) who starts divorce proceedings by making a petition for divorce.

Prejudice. In the context of this book, prejudice means an opinion or view held without proper study of the facts and that gives an unfair judgement.

Reconciliation. Not to be confused with **conciliation**. Conciliation seeks to mediate between a couple in dispute. Reconciliation seeks to bring a couple together again.

Residence order. Used by Children Act 1989 to determine which parent the child/children live(s) with.

Respondent. Opposite to **Petitioner** in a divorce case.

Separation. Usual term to describe the period when a married couple decide to live apart prior to instigating divorce proceedings.

Shared parenting. When two parents live apart but the children spend time with each parent on a regular basis. Both parents actively discuss the well-being of their children and make joint decisions.

Spouse. The husband or wife in a marriage.

Special needs. Wide range of disabilities and disadvantages that any individual, whether adult or child, can suffer. A universal term covering anything from dyslexia to Down's syndrome.

Splitting up. Common term for a relationship/marriage ending.

Statutory charge. The power a statutory authority (government body) can place on your property in order to regain money you owe after it is sold.

Stress. Term used to describe a situation when you find great difficulty with coping. A state that everyone experiences and that causes confusion and anxiety which can lead to illness (physically and mental). Relaxation and talking to others about your problems are the recommended ways to tackle stress.

Will. A document that states how you want your belongings and assets distributed amongst your family and friends, or others such as charities, in the event of your death. A lone parent would also nominate who will be the guardian and carer of their children and how they wish their children to be cared for. Usually one or more persons are nominated as executors of the will. These executors are people you know and trust to carry out your wishes.

Without prejudice. Most solicitors' letters carry this phrase at the top and, if you write your own, you should consider using it. This means that anything mentioned in the letter cannot be made known to the court, unless it is with the consent of both parties.

Index

How To Books provide practical help on a large range of topics. They are available through all good bookshops or can be ordered direct from the distributors. Just tick the titles you want and complete the form on the following page.

___ Apply to an Industrial Tribunal (£7.99)
___ Applying for a Job (£7.99)
___ Applying for a United States Visa (£15.99)
___ Be a Freelance Journalist (£8.99)
___ Be a Freelance Secretary (£8.99)
___ Be a Local Councillor (£8.99)
___ Be an Effective School Governor (£9.99)
___ Become a Freelance Sales Agent (£9.99)
___ Become an Au Pair (£8.99)
___ Buy & Run a Shop (£8.99)
___ Buy & Run a Small Hotel (£8.99)
___ Cash from your Computer (£9.99)
___ Career Planning for Women (£8.99)
___ Choosing a Nursing Home (£8.99)
___ Claim State Benefits (£9.99)
___ Communicate at Work (£7.99)
___ Conduct Staff Appraisals (£7.99)
___ Conducting Effective Interviews (£8.99)
___ Copyright & Law for Writers (£8.99)
___ Counsel People at Work (£7.99)
___ Creating a Twist in the Tale (£8.99)
___ Creative Writing (£9.99)
___ Critical Thinking for Students (£8.99)
___ Do Voluntary Work Abroad (£8.99)
___ Do Your Own Advertising (£8.99)
___ Do Your Own PR (£8.99)
___ Doing Business Abroad (£9.99)
___ Emigrate (£9.99)
___ Employ & Manage Staff (£8.99)
___ Find Temporary Work Abroad (£8.99)
___ Finding a Job in Canada (£9.99)
___ Finding a Job in Computers (£8.99)
___ Finding a Job in New Zealand (£9.99)
___ Finding a Job with a Future (£8.99)
___ Finding Work Overseas (£9.99)
___ Freelance DJ-ing (£8.99)
___ Get a Job Abroad (£10.99)
___ Get a Job in America (£9.99)
___ Get a Job in Australia (£9.99)
___ Get a Job in Europe (£9.99)
___ Get a Job in France (£9.99)
___ Get a Job in Germany (£9.99)
___ Get a Job in Hotels and Catering (£8.99)
___ Get a Job in Travel & Tourism (£8.99)
___ Get into Films & TV (£8.99)
___ Get into Radio (£8.99)
___ Get That Job (£6.99)
___ Getting your First Job (£8.99)
___ Going to University (£8.99)
___ Helping your Child to Read (£8.99)
___ Investing in People (£8.99)
___ Invest in Stocks & Shares (£8.99)

___ Keep Business Accounts (£7.99)
___ Know Your Rights at Work (£8.99)
___ Know Your Rights: Teachers (£6.99)
___ Live & Work in America (£9.99)
___ Live & Work in Australia (£12.99)
___ Live & Work in Germany (£9.99)
___ Live & Work in Greece (£9.99)
___ Live & Work in Italy (£8.99)
___ Live & Work in New Zealand (£9.99)
___ Live & Work in Portugal (£9.99)
___ Live & Work in Spain (£7.99)
___ Live & Work in the Gulf (£9.99)
___ Living & Working in Britain (£8.99)
___ Living & Working in China (£9.99)
___ Living & Working in Hong Kong (£10.99)
___ Living & Working in Israel (£10.99)
___ Living & Working in Japan (£8.99)
___ Living & Working in Saudi Arabia (£12.99)
___ Living & Working in the Netherlands (£9.99)
___ Lose Weight & Keep Fit (£6.99)
___ Make a Wedding Speech (£7.99)
___ Making a Complaint (£8.99)
___ Manage a Sales Team (£8.99)
___ Manage an Office (£8.99)
___ Manage Computers at Work (£8.99)
___ Manage People at Work (£8.99)
___ Manage Your Career (£8.99)
___ Managing Budgets & Cash Flows (£9.99)
___ Managing Meetings (£8.99)
___ Managing Your Personal Finances (£8.99)
___ Market Yourself (£8.99)
___ Master Book-Keeping (£8.99)
___ Mastering Business English (£8.99)
___ Master GCSE Accounts (£8.99)
___ Master Languages (£8.99)
___ Master Public Speaking (£8.99)
___ Obtaining Visas & Work Permits (£9.99)
___ Organising Effective Training (£9.99)
___ Pass Exams Without Anxiety (£7.99)
___ Pass That Interview (£6.99)
___ Plan a Wedding (£7.99)
___ Prepare a Business Plan (£8.99)
___ Publish a Book (£9.99)
___ Publish a Newsletter (£9.99)
___ Raise Funds & Sponsorship (£7.99)
___ Rent & Buy Property in France (£9.99)
___ Rent & Buy Property in Italy (£9.99)
___ Retire Abroad (£8.99)
___ Return to Work (£7.99)
___ Run a Local Campaign (£6.99)
___ Run a Voluntary Group (£8.99)
___ Sell Your Business (£9.99)

___ Selling into Japan (£14.99)
___ Setting up Home in Florida (£9.99)
___ Spend a Year Abroad (£8.99)
___ Start a Business from Home (£7.99)
___ Start a New Career (£6.99)
___ Starting to Manage (£8.99)
___ Starting to Write (£8.99)
___ Start Word Processing (£8.99)
___ Start Your Own Business (£8.99)
___ Study Abroad (£8.99)
___ Study & Learn (£7.99)
___ Study & Live in Britain (£7.99)
___ Studying at University (£8.99)
___ Studying for a Degree (£8.99)
___ Successful Grandparenting (£8.99)
___ Successful Mail Order Marketing (£9.99)
___ Successful Single Parenting (£8.99)
___ Survive at College (£4.99)
___ Survive Divorce (£8.99)
___ Surviving Redundancy (£8.99)
___ Take Care of Your Heart (£5.99)
___ Taking in Students (£8.99)
___ Taking on Staff (£8.99)
___ Taking Your A-Levels (£8.99)
___ Teach Abroad (£8.99)
___ Teach Adults (£8.99)
___ Teaching Someone to Drive (£8.99)
___ Travel Round the World (£8.99)
___ Use a Library (£6.99)

___ Use the Internet (£9.99)
___ Winning Consumer Competitions (£8.99)
___ Winning Presentations (£8.99)
___ Work from Home (£8.99)
___ Work in an Office (£7.99)
___ Work in Retail (£8.99)
___ Work with Dogs (£8.99)
___ Working Abroad (£14.99)
___ Working as a Holiday Rep (£9.99)
___ Working in Japan (£10.99)
___ Working in Photography (£8.99)
___ Working in the Gulf (£10.99)
___ Working on Contract Worldwide (£9.99)
___ Working on Cruise Ships (£9.99)
___ Write a CV that Works (£7.99)
___ Write a Press Release (£9.99)
___ Write a Report (£8.99)
___ Write an Assignment (£8.99)
___ Write an Essay (£7.99)
___ Write & Sell Computer Software (£9.99)
___ Write Business Letters (£8.99)
___ Write for Publication (£8.99)
___ Write for Television (£8.99)
___ Write Your Dissertation (£8.99)
___ Writing a Non Fiction Book (£8.99)
___ Writing & Selling a Novel (£8.99)
___ Writing & Selling Short Stories (£8.99)
___ Writing Reviews (£8.99)
___ Your Own Business in Europe (£12.99)

To: Plymbridge Distributors Ltd, Plymbridge House, Estover Road, Plymouth PL6 7PZ.
Customer Services Tel: (01752) 202301. Fax: (01752) 202331.

Please send me copies of the titles I have indicated. Please add postage & packing
(UK £1, Europe including Eire, £2, World £3 airmail).

☐ I enclose cheque/PO payable to Plymbridge Distributors Ltd for £ [   ]

☐ Please charge to my ☐ MasterCard, ☐ Visa, ☐ AMEX card.

Account No. [| | | | | | | | | | | | | | |]

Card Expiry Date [|] 19 [   ]   ☎ **Credit Card orders may be faxed or phoned.**

Customer Name (CAPITALS) ....

Address ....

.... Postcode ....

Telephone .... Signature ....

Every effort will be made to despatch your copy as soon as possible but to avoid possible
disappointment please allow up to 21 days for despatch time (42 days if overseas). Prices
and availability are subject to change without notice.   CODE BPA